# EXPERT SYSTEMS:
## Strategic Implications and Applications

**ELLIS HORWOOD BOOKS IN INFORMATION TECHNOLOGY**
*General Editor:* Dr. JOHN M. M. PINKERTON, Principal, McLean Pinkerton
Associates, Surrey, (formerly Manager of Strategic Requirements,
International Computers Limited)

**A PRACTICAL APPROACH TO EXPERT SYSTEMS IN BUSINESS**
M. BARRETT, Expertech Ltd., and A. C. BEEREL, Director, Lysia Ltd.
**EXPERT SYSTEMS: STRATEGIC IMPLICATIONS AND APPLICATIONS**
A. C. BEEREL, Director, Lysia Ltd., London
**SOFTWARE ENGINEERING ENVIRONMENTS**
P. BRERETON, University of Keele
**INTERPRETING ANAPHORS IN NATURAL LANGUAGE TEXTS**
D. CARTER, University Engineering Department, Cambridge
**PRACTICAL MACHINE TRANSLATION**
D. CLARKE and U. MAGNUSSON-MURRAY, Department of Applied Computing and
Mathematics, Cranfield Institute of Technology, Bedford
**KNOWLEDGE-BASED EXPERT SYSTEMS IN INDUSTRY**
J. KRIZ, Head of AI Group, Brown Boveri Research Center, Switzerland
**ADVANCED INFORMATION TECHNOLOGY**
J. M. M. PINKERTON, Principal, McLean Pinkerton, Esher
**BUILDING EXPERT SYSTEMS: Cognitive Emulation**
P. E. SLATTER, Product Designer, Telecomputing plc, Oxford
**SPEECH AND LANGUAGE-BASED COMMUNICATION WITH MACHINES**
Editor: J. A. WATERWORTH, British Telecom Research Laboratories, Ipswich

# EXPERT SYSTEMS:
## Strategic Implications and Applications

ANNABEL C. BEEREL
Director, Lysia Limited, London

**ELLIS HORWOOD LIMITED**
Publishers · Chichester

Halsted Press: a division of
**JOHN WILEY & SONS**
New York · Chichester · Brisbane · Toronto

First published in 1987 by
**ELLIS HORWOOD LIMITED**
Market Cross House, Cooper Street,
Chichester, West Sussex, PO19 1EB, England
*The publisher's colophon is reproduced from James Gillison's drawing of the ancient Market Cross, Chichester.*

**Distributors:**

*Australia and New Zealand:*
JACARANDA WILEY LIMITED
GPO Box 859, Brisbane, Queensland 4001, Australia

*Canada:*
JOHN WILEY & SONS CANADA LIMITED
22 Worcester Road, Rexdale, Ontario, Canada

*Europe and Africa:*
JOHN WILEY & SONS LIMITED
Baffins Lane, Chichester, West Sussex, England

*North and South America and the rest of the world:*
Halsted Press: a division of
JOHN WILEY & SONS
605 Third Avenue, New York, NY 10158, USA

© 1987 A. C. Beerel/Ellis Horwood Limited

**British Library Cataloguing in Publication Data**
Beerel, Annabel, C.
Expert systems: strategic implications and applications. —
(Ellis Horwood books in information technology).
1. Expert systems (Computer science)
I. Title
006.3'3    QA76.9.E95

**Library of Congress Card No.** 87–18427

ISBN 0–7458–0251–6 (Ellis Horwood Limited)
ISBN 0–470–20974–7 (Halsted Press)

Printed in Great Britain by R. J. Acford, Chichester

# Contents

# Preface

There are three basic philosophies underlying this book, the first and most important being that we are moving towards a knowledge-based society. The second premise is that there will be renewed recognition of people as knowledge workers. Thirdly, information technology (notably expert systems) will play a major role in harnessing inherent knowledge to the strategic advantage of all organisations.

The move towards a knowledge-based society has already begun. This is evidenced by the importance placed on information and expertise in establishing comparative advantages. Knowledge is the new commodity being traded. This book sets out to prepare managers to take advantage of this new revolution.

The emphasis on knowledge has replaced the spotlight on man. After all, knowledge resides in man. Hitherto it could only be created and transmitted by him. The new challenge is to encapsulate, expand and transfer knowledge by means of an intelligent machine. Far from demeaning man, this will engender a new respect for the human thought process and the expertise that each and every individual holds within his own domain.

It is the unique knowledge of the expert in every domain that can be potentially harnessed in a thinking machine. The new technology is known as expert systems, an offspring of Artificial Intelligence.

Linking the strategic commodity, knowledge, with the new information technology, expert systems, can provide new strategic advantages. This book discusses why and how.

Annabel C. Beerel
*London 1987*

# Acknowledgements

My sincere thanks to Dr Lilly Evans who painstakingly read my manuscript and offered valuable comments and encouragement.

A special thank you to my publisher, Sue Horwood, with whom it has been a pleasure to work.

# Introduction

This book brings together the needs and pursuits of management and the ways in which the latest technology can be used to strategic advantage in those activities. It is about the strategic implications and applications of expert systems: it should be read by strategic, technical and operational management and by technologists in every field. Academics and scientists carrying out research in all areas of AI, particularly expert systems, will gain by being exposed to the insights presented here.

There is no forerunner to this book, and at this stage little empirical evidence of how expert systems can be harnessed into the strategic armoury of the organisation. A lot of what follows can be correctly argued as being anticipatory — however, events will continue to move forward at a rapid pace.

This is a book about expert systems for management. It is primarily aimed at those who are actively involved in managing a particular function within an organisation, those who interact with business managers, e.g. consultants and technologists, and those who aspire to become managers.

The well known theories of excellence, corporate culture, competitive advantage and leadership styles will be discussed but not rediscovered or reproven here. Instead this book will show how Expert Systems can be used as another tool in moving these concepts from the realm of theory to everyday profitable practice.

Surely it is fair to say that we live in a turbulent world? A world in which countries, corporates and individuals need to resort to new approaches in order to survive with any kind of equanimity. Turbulence denotes a state of commotion characterised by irregular behaviour, volatile trends and new patterns of both attack and defence. In the commercial world, executives and corporate managers are finding that

— the future is highly uncertain
— the environment is full of frightening rather than delightful surprises

— historical strategies can no longer be blindly repeated but are increasingly suspect
— growth no longer extrapolates in the same direction or with the same momentum as in the past
— profitability is no longer necessarily a function of growth
— human behaviour is not only demonstrating greater complexity as a result of greater human freedom, but human needs and motivation appear to require more complicated solutions.

How then should management respond? What insights, education and skills do managers require in order to lead organisations to long-term success for the wealth and the betterment to all concerned?

In order to address some of the challenges outlined, the past number of years have seen a rash of management books entitled in some way '...Excellence' or '...Strategy'. A global preoccupation has evolved whereby governments and corporates are driven by the need to create and sustain an acceptable competitive edge. The rationale underlying this, is that it will lead to an improved quality of life for the people of the country or corporate concerned. The search is fostering new relationships and new scientific and technological developments. Governments and corporates are not alone in the search for a better lifestyle. Individuals are taking their own initiative in this direction.

This book does not intend to validate or refute these observations. What is does support is that such a movement is needed and will inevitably evolve. A search for truth and peace is surely a search for knowledge. What knowledge is will be addressed in Part I of this book; however, the deep philosophical discussions surrounding knowledge will be left to the philosophers.

'The Japanese are planning the miracle product. It will come not from their mines, their wells, their fields, or even their seas. It comes instead from their brains. The miracle product is knowledge, and the Japanese are planning to package and sell it the way other nations package and sell energy, food, or manufactured goods.' (Edward A Feigenbaum and Pamela McCorduck, *The Fifth Generation*, Pan Books.)

The Japanese have committed some $1 billion to this exotic dream — it is their belief that knowledge is power. The goal is to develop computers that are intelligent, machines which will be able to learn, associate, assimilate, make inferences and thus arrive at decisions. They are designed to mimic human reasoning and thus intelligence. The Japanese have even set up an Institute for New Generation Computer Technology (ICOT) which is totally dedicated to this *nationwide* project.

Artificial Intelligence (AI) is the new phase of computer technology (fifth generation computing) concerned with making machines carry out tasks which, had they been performed by humans would have been deemed to require intelligence. Expert system applications, as part of AI, are those that perform highly specialised activities which are normally considered to require human expertise. They are similar to human experts in that they can justify their conclusions and recall the knowledge that they applied to the problem.

Very little, if anything has been written about the strategic implications of expert systems for managers. Managers are preoccupied with the facets of their businesses which they hold to be strategic. Having a good strategy or being a good strategist denotes a semblance of power and of having great foresight and anticipatory skills. If a technique or tool exists which has the potential for enabling managers to heighten their strategic skills they feel very positively inclined towards investigating that potential in some depth.

Most of the literature on Artificial Intelligence (AI) and expert systems has been addressed to those interested in computing and systems technology. The level of the address also assumes a high degree of technical expertise and hands-on experience. The ambit of the knowledge required of a successful manager is continually widening and demanding increased systems awareness and understanding. It is probable that most managers especially senior executives, might wish for a better understanding of computer technology. Most managers possibly do not know what, if anything, they should do about expert systems.

Strategy is all about problem solving and decision making in an unstructured situation which contains a high degree of uncertainty. The greater the knowledge, hindsight and information the strategist can apply to the problem, the more astute he is likely to be and therefore the greater the chance that his decision will be a correct one.

One of the first applications of expert systems was that of the strategic and masterful game of chess. Chess has a set of rules and a distinctive goal of 'checkmate' which both beginners and champions (world experts) alike, set out to achieve. The challenge is how best, i.e. most effectively, to attain the goal and thus to win. The players use far more than just the rules of manipulating the pieces on the chess-board to achieve their aim. They incorporate hindsight (what they did right or wrong last time); they use anticipation (they second-guess what the opponent will do); they use innate intuition and experience along with the psychological skills of attack and defence.

Today's world leaders and executives are in a similar situation. They face not only the challenge of achieving their goal but they have to harness the resources of their organisation, corporation or community in order to attain a strategic edge akin to 'check'.

In Part I (The Strategic Implications of Expert Systems) we will discuss the search for knowledge, the understanding of how we arrive at decisions; our strategic initiatives and the new technology and how this new integration will influence our lives.

The great contribution of expert systems will be to unite people, in the office, shopfloor or executive suite in the pursuit of knowledge. There will be new acknowledgement that people are valuable.

Part II will explore the problems and challenges of identifying meaningful applications; enlisting the co-operation of suitable experts; motivating a business proposal for expert system development and understanding the role of the knowledge engineer. It highlights how appropriate applications can be developed as a result of the analysis of the critical success factors of the organisation.

Part III is a practical guide to getting started. It explains how the organisation can prepare itself to exploit expert system applications and monitor the progress of development and implementation.

For the sake of fluency the generic term of his or him has been used and should be readily replaced with hers or her.

# Glossary

| | |
|---|---|
| **algorithm** | a formal procedure which is guaranteed to produce correct or optimal solutions. |
| **Artificial Intelligence** | a subsection of computer science concerned with developing programs that in some way imitate human intelligent behaviour. |
| **combinatorial explosion** | where the number of possible alternative combinations get very large and can potentially reach infinity. |
| **control rules** | these rules govern the sequence of inference by giving the system special instructions. |
| **CFF** | critical failure factor. |
| **CSF** | critical success factor. |
| **cognitive style** | is the manner in which an individual perceives data and formulates knowledge from the assimilated data. |
| **deskilling** | the apparent transference of specialised skills from man to machine. |
| **domain expert** | a human expert, recognised as such, who provides know-how to the system in a narrow area of specialism. |
| **Decision Support System (DSS)** | a computer system designed to provide information deemed relevant to the making of a decision. DSS provide support to the decision maker but do not replace him. |

| | |
|---|---|
| **DP** | data processing. |
| **ES** | Expert System. |
| **Expert System** | a computer program that uses expert knowledge to reach a level of performance akin to that achievable by highly skilled experts. In these programs the knowledge is presented symbolically rather than numerically. The system is designed to address complex problems and to explain its reasoning processes. |
| **Expert System Building Tool** | a programming language and/or support packages used to build and test the expert system. |
| **heuristic** | a rule of thumb or simplification that limits the search for solutions. |
| **inference engine** | the inference engine processes the domain knowledge included in the system to reach new conclusions. It is realised by special software in a computer. |
| **inferencing** | forming logical conclusions from given facts or premises. |
| **interpreter** | a part of the inference engine that decides how to apply the domain knowledge. |
| **know-how** | know-how is practical knowledge gained by exposure and experience. |
| **knowledge acquisition** | the process of extracting relevant knowledge from human experts so that it can be included in the expert system knowledge base. |
| **knowledge base** | the information held in an expert system that constitutes its expertise. |
| **knowledge engineer** | the person who designs and builds the expert system assisted by the domain expert. |
| **knowledge engineering** | the process of designing and building an expert system. |
| **Knowledge information processing systems (KIPS)** | computer systems that incorporate large amounts of knowledge rather than algorithms. |
| **knowledge representation** | a way of structuring knowledge in a manner that suitably replicates human problem solving. |

| | |
|---|---|
| **payoff** | the anticipated benefit (in both quantitative and qualitative terms) as a result of a course of action. |
| **ROI** | return on investment. |
| **Search** | the process of examining the set of possible solutions to a problem in order to find an acceptable solution. |
| **soft costs** | costs not readily itemised or quantified as they are covert and/or inherent costs. |
| **symbolic computing** | the programming of a computer by using symbols rather than numbers. |
| **symbolic reasoning** | problem solving by manipulating symbols that stand for problem concepts. |
| **QCC** | Quality Control Circles. |

# Part I

## The Strategic Implications of Expert Systems

# 1

# The business environment today

The business environment today is fiercely competitive. Any new idea. process or technique that will provide management with the means of gaining a competitive edge, no matter how small, is worthy of serious exploration. This book is about a new technique which has the potential for providing a *substantial* competitive edge. Realising this potential can only be achieved if it is used as a tool that can help managers address their real day to day problems. Before we discuss the details with regard to this new tool, the Expert System, it is appropriate to discuss the challenges facing management.

## 1.1   THE PREOCCUPATION OF MANAGEMENT IN THE 1980S AND 1990S

The challenges facing management today are far more complex than those faced in previous decades. Why is this so? Is it because the world is apparently smaller and increasingly interdependent? Is it because of the advancement of science and technology which appears to have no constraints? Is it because intensive (maybe excessive) competition has arbitraged away most of our profits? Is it because players have misused the opportunities presented by open economies? Or is it because the world's *stakeholders* are exerting pressure for their self-perceived rights?

The past decade has seen a plethora of management books, conferences and seminars all aspiring to support the beleaguered manager in this tumultuous environment. Managers have been bombarded with acronyms, mnemonics, matrices, slogans and other forms of analytical tools. They have been rigorously put through their paces on leadership, management styles, strategic planning, competitor analysis and the management of change. Is it not perhaps a suitable time to stand back for a moment and ask ourselves *why* management seeks such extensive training and support?

*Organisations want to be successful*
*People want to be successful*

Successful organisations are usually a function of successful teamwork. People sometimes feel that they are personally successful if their organisations are successful — but this is not always necessarily so.

How can one define organisational success?

- is it the largest organisation?
  - in terms of assets?
  - in terms of people?
- is it the most profitable organisation?
  - per capita?
  - as a ratio of capital employed?
- is it the most stable organisation?
  - in terms of employee stability?
  - consistent earnings?

Clearly there is no one single measure for success on which all people will agree.

Further we must not forget that success is a relative concept and that success can only be measured in the context of what it is being measured against. The pursuits of management can be summarised by proposing that the management of an organisation seeks to out-perform the management of other organisations by paying careful attention to

**Corporate culture**
**Competitive advantage**
**Cost of capital**

It is held that it is management's strategic vision and decision-making ability that will mould and develop the organisation into the *ultimately* successful one — where employees and management alike, have the promise of prosperity and the freedom to share in it.

Figure 1.1 endeavours to encapsulate the thrust of management thinking and the theories as *often* preached and *sometimes* practised. The managerial aspects listed under the 3Cs are not mentioned in any order of priority. Also, none of the concepts or ideas are mutually exclusive.

**Corporate culture**   The importance of a healthy corporate culture is being stressed over and over again. All the 'Excellent' books (In Search of Excellence, A Journey to Excellence, Creating Excellence, Roots of Excellence ... and so on) emphasise that a congruent, consistent, value-driven corporate culture is a necessary foundation to outstanding organisational performance. The ingredients for a positive cultural environment include standards such as vision, commitment, strategic thinking, values and congruence, consistency and appropriate leadership styles.

| Corporate Culture | Vision |
| | Strategic thinking |
| | Commitment |
| | Values and congruence |
| | Consistency |
| | Leadership style |
| | |
| Competitive Advantage | Differentiation |
| | Targeting markets |
| | Understanding customers |
| | Quality |
| | Vision |
| | Commitment |
| | |
| Cost of Capital | Efficiency |
| | Learning curve |
| | Corporate marketing |
| | Gearing |
| | Vision |
| | Commitment |

Fig. 1.1

**Vision**   It is vitally important for management to have and to be able to demonstrate visionary thinking. Vision denotes being able to mentally journey into the future in an enlightened and penetrating manner. It means being able to be anticipative in an insightful way. The visionary welcomes the future as he can respond to it with perspicacity, and he typically sees it full of opportunity and challenge. Owing to his cagacious insights his planning horizon is long-term rather than short-term.

**Strategic thinking**   A healthy corporate culture is fostered by elements of strategic thinking at all levels of the organisation. Strategic thinking is that ability to out-think, outplan and outplay the adversary. The ability to think strategically is enhanced by the existence of visionary management. Well-thought-out strategies decidedly help to determine success. The ability to think and act strategically needs to be inculcated within every manager and should not be left to the ivory tower corporate planners. Too often managers do not reflect sufficiently on the continuous fight for strategic advantage. The fight consists of both *battles* and *wars*. Surely managers want to win the *war*?

   Instead management focuses on winning every battle. If competitors cut prices, they cut prices; if competitors spend millions on advertising, management responds similarly; if competitors open up production plants in Singapore, they open up production plants in Korea. Is there one general who won every battle, never retreated to firmer ground, never drew the enemy on only to envelop them in devastating pincer movements?

   Strategic thinking is the ability to distinguish the battle from the war; to insightfully use people, resources and time to take advantage of strengths and opportunities and to judiciously make short-term sacrifices in prudent anticipation of things to come.

---

**Battles and wars**
Many managers

- do not know the difference between battles and wars
- treat every battle as a war
- seldom know which they have lost until it is too late

---

**Commitment**   Corporate culture should 'reek' of almost fanatical commitment. Managers should be committed to the organisation, to the employees and to their strategic plans. The commitment should be firm without resulting in intransigence. Managers are often guilty of treating acquiescence as commitment. These are two very different things. Having given the go-ahead to a project is very different to actually feeling personal commitment to see it through.

**Values and congruence**   Culture is all about value systems. Building culture into the organisation requires application of the softer management skills. All of the successful organisations (IBM, DEC, Toyota, 3M) evidence some sharing of common values. These values can be either highly organisationally oriented, e.g. care for the customer, or they can be more widely oriented, e.g. people come first — both the customer and the employee. Commitment and deference to the value system unite the organisational community. The value system adopted by the organisation needs to be congruent to the type of organisation, the type and style of management and the employees. If congruence is lacking, in that the value system is inappropriate or in conflict with other more respected values, tension will develop and eventually undermine both the value system and any culture building that is taking place.

**Consistency**   Being consistent in one's values, commitment and behaviour has great worth. Approaching managerial tasks and challenges in a consistent and committed manner enhances organisational stability, supports the corporate culture and leads to greater equity in relations between both customers and staff.

**Leadership style**   Tomes have been written about leadership styles. Academics have developed grids (notably *The Managerial Grid III*, Blake and Mouton, Gulf Publishing Company, 1985), games, check-lists and matrix analyses (to mention but a few) in order to evaluate and assess leadership styles. Whatever the leadership style of an organisation, it should be appropriate to the type of organisation and the stage in its life cycle. Effective leadership will positively reinforce corporate culture by engendering strategic thinking, commitment and trust.

As stressed earlier, corporate culture, the concept and the building thereof, is receiving avid attention. This book is not about summarising the myriad [of] books that already exist on this theme. It is also not intended to astound the reader with 'quotable quotes' from eminent business men, leaders or academics. This book is about another, new, exciting and different tool that will help managers to *develop* and *enhance* their corporate culture. This tool is called expert systems.

**Competitive advantage**   This is our modern term for survival in the long-run. Be it in the classroom, on the field, in our social groups or between organisations the pressures of competition are always with us. Some organisations, depending on their contingent of people respond well to the competitive challenge — and then some do not! As we know, competitive advantage is about developing a distinctive organisational competence in the market-place; creating barriers to entry and stimulating customer loyalty. Establishing and sustaining a competitive advantage is one of the most tortuous tasks facing management today. Being able to respond to the challenge demands not only a better understanding of our competitors but a more insightful understanding of ourselves. Chapter 6 is solely devoted to competitive advantage and expert systems, therefore the subject will only be introduced here.

**Differentiation**   Most organisations seek to differentiate their products or services from their competitors in order to have a distinctive offering that appeals to the discriminating consumer and encourages customer loyalty. Differentiation can manifest itself in the quality, in the price, in the packaging, in the delivery or in the promotion of the product or service. The role of technology in product/service differentiation cannot be over-estimated.

**Targeting markets**   The concept of carefully targeting markets is now a well established one. The importance of market segmentation lies in focusing the products/services and resources of an organisation into a market of customers with certain (preresearched) homogeneous needs which these products/services seek to satisfy. Targeted markets result in better understanding of customer needs, improved concentration of the organisation's market planning and the opportunity to develop entry barriers.

**Understanding customers**   Many writers of management books postulate that the keystone of organisational strategy is the understanding of the organisation's customers' needs. A devotion to the customer is one of the eight attributes attributed to excellent companies in *In Search of Excellence*. This devotion manifests itself in putting the customer first, paying attention to detail and providing consistent quality and reliability.

**Quality**   Quality is a relative concept. Gaining competitive advantage is most often achieved by providing products/services that have a *relatively* higher standard of quality than those of the competition. The quality emphasis could be on the ingredients, the packaging, the image portrayal, the distribution, the after-sales service or the pure efficiency with which the product or service performs its function. Again the role of technology cannot be over-emphasised. The Japanese have led the drive for relative quality. The Germans and Swiss have always been fairly good at it. The other Newly Industrialised Countries (NICs) are learning fast. Consumer sophistication is driving the competitive response of a relative quality for the price. Only those organisations that understand their customers really well will achieve accurate comprehension of the quality that is expected.

**Vision**   The concept of vision appears yet again under competitive advantage. A major requirement of the successful organisation is for management to have foresight with regard to their markets, customers and competitors. Visionary management is usually good at anticipating market changes, can influence and preempt customer needs in favour of the organisation, and of course, second guess the competition. Vision is required in order to sustain that long-term view, to encourage healthy risk-taking and in order to have the courage to embark on long-term investments and wise research and development.

**Commitment**   Commitment, like vision is a critical requirement of successful management. Commitment must exude from the organisation. Customers must feel that the organisation is committed to fulfilling their needs; the industry (i.e. associate and competitor organisations) want to feel that the organisation is committed to its avowed promises and competitors *need* to know that the organisation is committed to its cause. Commitment breeds confidence and success — both of which are mutually reinforcing.

The roads to *competitive advantage* are many. Some are long and arduous, some short and exciting. Some of the paths taken are windy, interrupted and inconsistent while others are direct, focused and straight. Understanding which path will make for the most effective competitive advantage which lies within the organisation's abilities and time frame is unique to each situation. This book does not intend to cover ground well covered by prestigious authors on competitive strategies or competitive analysis: the intention is to investigate a new management tool and its potential for gaining and sustaining competitive advantage — *Expert Systems*.

**Cost of capital**   The cost of capital to an organisation is ofter seen as an adjunct to attaining competitive advantage. One can give credence to the point that being able to optimise the organisation's cost of capital is an important element of competitive advantage. This can be identified as a separate (but overlapping) element of managerial pursuit. The cost of capital to an organisation is a far more complex concept than whether the organisation borrows at 2% or 3% above base rate.

The cost of capital reflects the financial (and creditor) community's perception of risk, expectation of performance and to a large extent recognition of the image of the organisation. The cost of capital of an organisation is largely dependent on its track record, its cash generating capability, its corporate marketing, the perceived corporate culture and its ability to exploit a competitive advantage.

**Efficiency**   Achieving the organisational objectives is being effective. Doing this at a better than average input to output ratio is being efficient. Efficiency really means how little (or how much) effort does one need to invest in order to gain an optimal return (or output). Evidence of being efficient is another accolade bestowed upon *excellent* companies. It is true to say that all of us strive to be more efficient in our lives. Scarce resources, pressures on time and the ingenuity of scientists and technologists has heightened our understanding of efficient markets and the benefits of a well communicated financial strategy.

**Learning curve**   The benefits of the learning curve were pointed out to us after the Second World War with the increased production efficiency and labour costs savings resulting from mass production. However, it has taken the Japanese to push home the point that *managing* the learning curve effect can provide a distinct strategic advantage. The basic premise of the learning curve is that labour hours decrease in a definite pattern as labour operations are repeated. The pattern is as follows: each time *cumulative* quantities are doubled, the *cumulative average* hours per unit will be reduced by some constant percentage — usually ranging between 10 and 40%. If the rate of reduction is 20%, the curve is referred to as the 80% learning curve. Improving operating efficiency has a direct effect on the organisation's cost of capital. Better asset management results in shorter trading cycles, a better cash generating ability and consequently better returns.

**Corporate marketing**   This is a movement that has taken off in the United States. Corporate marketing is that activity which promotes the corporate as a whole — it is deemed to be more than publicity and public relations. The primary objective of corporate marketing is to positively promote the organisation, as a whole, to both current and potential shareholders.

The end result of a corporate marketing campaign should reflect itself positively in that organisation's share price (or its overall value if it is unquoted). As we all know, a high share price and a high *price/earnings* ratio is the key stock market indicator of how favourably the stock market views management's efforts. Provided of course that the P/E ratio is not totally over the top due to some market aberration, the cost of capital will benefit up to a point.

**Gearing**   This is no place to discuss the theories of Modigliani and Miller or to analyse in detail the effects of gearing. Suffice it to say that the more highly geared the organisation, normally the greater the perceived risk. When things are going well it is beneficial to be highly geared. If the market turns, gearing can place an organisation in dire straits very rapidly. Investors and borrowers typically like *more* return with *less* risk (see Fig. 1.2).

They also do not welcome surprises. Managing the organisation's gearing

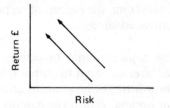

Fig. 1.2.

levels in a prudent manner is critical to the financial strategy of a business. If investors or lenders perceive high risks they will demand greater returns and *up* goes the cost of capital.

**Vision**   Management that can demonstrate that they are realistic visionaries will gain the confidence of lenders and investors. Visionaries are inclined to take healthy risks. Owing to their longer time and planning horizons they will invest in the future, they will sponsor research and development, they are likely to nurture those loose–tight properties (an attribute accorded excellent companies in *In Search of Excellence*) and to encourage intrapreneurship. The visionary organisation is likely to get the benefit of supportive financiers. A good example of visionary management would seem to be Glaxo Plc led by Chairman Paul Girolami. According to a report in *Management Today*, February 1987, Glaxo is now the most profitable pharmaceutical company in the world with the phenomenal return on capital employed of over 55% — how do they do it?

**Commitment**   Investors and lenders like to see managerial commitment. As mentioned earlier commitment fosters trust. The greater the trust, the less the perceived risk. The more favourable the financing, naturally the easier to achieve better than market average returns, and thus the cheaper the finance — a self-fulfilling prophecy.

Theories on cost of capital abound. Only the essence of some of the theory and how it is practised has been outlined.

What is important is how expert systems can act as another tool in positively managing the cost of capital of an organisation.

---

**The eight attributes of excellent companies**

- A bias for action
- Close to the customer
- Autonomy and entrepreneurship
- Productivity through people
- Hands-on, value driven
- Stick to the knitting
- Simple form, lean staff
- Simultaneous loose–tight properties

---

Extract from Peters and Waterman, *In Search of Excellence*, (Harper & Row, New York).

## 1.2   MOTIVATION

It is commonly recognised that self-motivation is the most fruitful and sustainable motivation. If a climate exists which *encourages*, *reinforces* and *rewards* self-motivation, people will be spurred on to increased productivity and creativity. Management needs to create a climate where

— Work is meaningful (a variety of skills are called upon and the individual experiences identity with his tasks and feels that they are significant in the contribution to overall organisational objectives).
— The individual gains regular and speedy feedback from his tasks (i.e. experience of results) as well as from those he works with and for.
— The individual has a feeling of responsibility for the outcome of his efforts. He needs to have a certain feeling of freedom and independence, in which he can exercise a certain amount of discretion.

These are most commonly described as the requisite conditions for sparking internal motivation.

Maslow, Herzberg, McGregor, Mintzberg and others have plenty to say on motivation.

We all agree that we would like to lead and/or be part of a highly motivated organisation! This will not only help us at work, but also at home and at play.

There could be a new technique of enhancing self-motivation — expert systems.

## 1.3   WOULD YOU BE INTERESTED IN?

A tool that could

- promote visionary, strategic thinking
- improve decision making
- assist you in analysing your own decision-making process
- aid management in identifying the real experts within the organisation
- engage all functions of the organisation in becoming more innovative
- promote shared values where these exist
- encourage the deployment of 'self'
- engender a bias for action
- spur on autonomy and entrepreneurship
- assist in achieving productivity *through* people
- incorporate the latest information technology into your strategic armoury

- assist in managerial plans for succession

A technique for

- promoting commitment and consistency
- building an in-house knowledge bank
- creating differentiation strategies
- developing an incremental, communal hindsight
- enhancing quality in a wholistic sense
- raising competitive barriers to entry
- influencing investor and borrower perception of the risks of your business
- getting closer to the customer
- gaining greater and faster benefits than the traditional learning curve effect
- motivating the right people at the right time
- focusing people on working smarter rather than harder
- developing the new strategic commodity — knowledge

# 2

# Expert systems as a management tool

It is a feat that a new, *relatively* unexplored tool can possibly achieve all of the things an organisation requires for success. Firstly it needs to be made very clear that expert systems *could* achieve some of these things, not that they *should*. Secondly, it will be a unique organisation that will experience *all* of the benefits mentioned in Chapter 1. It will also be a time-consuming process, whereby the organisation will have to be led through the management of change — refer to Chapter 14 (Preparing the Organisation for Expert Systems). The way expert systems are used in an organisation will greatly depend on management's vision, commitment, and strategic thinking ability. Success is definitely not guaranteed — this is not a 'wait'-watchers' book but a strategic players' book. If you are waiting for the future to arrive before you act, you will be living in the past!

It is vitally important to recognise in the early stages that:

---

Expert systems
- can never include common sense
- can never totally substitute for people
- cannot take the place of judgement (where there are qualitative or emotional issues — which is nearly always the case)
- are only as good as the expert knowledge included in the rule-base
- are only effective in a very narrow domain area
- are constrained by both the software and hardware, currently available on which to operate them
- should be considered as a *process* rather than a *results* oriented tool — refer to Chapter 4 — The Role of Knowledge in Strategic Decision-making.

---

If anything, Expert Systems will make people *more* important to the organisation, not less! — more of which in the ensuing chapters.

## 2.1   MANAGEMENT AND PRODUCTIVITY ENHANCEMENT

One of the greatest challenges facing management is that of managing people. Improving productivity of the workers in the organisation is an essential endeavour on which most management lay a great deal of emphasis. It is a well recognised fact that we all aspire to work smarter rather than harder! Establishing and sustaining competitive advantage depends largely on working smarter and all organisations would wish to achieve this. The new tool, expert systems, has its greatest value in that it provides people with an opportunity to enhance their performance. This will manifest itself differently in different people, depending on their involvement with the expert system and their willingness to participate.

Performance inprovements come about, among other things, as a result of:

- the opportunity to access expert advice at any time
- the ability to query the expert's reasoning, and to go over it time and time again in order to understand the underlying logic. No expert would have the time or the patience to be questioned in this fashion.
- the possibility of having an *aide-mémoire* which can provide expert guidance while performing a particular task.
- the ability to obtain consistent advice regardless of the emotional or political aspects surrounding the query. This again is unlikely to be attainable from a human expert who is often unable to be totally objective all of the time.
- the opportunity to change, amend and expand the rule-base so as to enhance the performance of the system. The person who has to opportunity of doing this will learn a great deal.

Expert systems are suitable for all tasks that require experience in order to perform them proficiently. Gaining experience is a time consuming, sometimes traumatic and often a very expensive process. Expert systems provide people with the opportunity of gaining experience at a fast rate with far less trauma and cost attached thereto. Further, as will be expanded upon in the ensuing chapter, expert systems are computer systems that encapsulate *knowledge*. This knowledge is far wider than that usually included in textbooks, manuals or training lectures. This knowledge is that of an *expert* in a specified field who enriches the system with his experience. This experience arises from actually performing a task and learning routes to success and pitfalls to avoid. It is this practical *know-how* which is to be harnessed into the knowledge-base of the system.

From management's perspective expert systems provide a potentially powerful tool that can quickly and efficiently upgrade the performance of employees. The problem for management is that (a) expert systems take a fairly long time to build and (b) that as with most performance improvement systems, the benefits are not easily quantifiable. The gains from a system are usually greatly evident with the benefit of hindsight. This does of course not help managers in applying for investment funds that are almost always well over-subscribed. Healthy investment decisions that require foresight and judicious risktaking are essential for every successful company. Expert systems and the investment decision will be expanded upon in Part II.

## 2.2   FORMS AND USES OF EXPERT SYSTEMS

Hopefully your appetite has been whetted, your intellect challenged and your visionary aptitude stirred sufficiently to want to understand what expert systems might be able to do for you. In order to get a better feel for this it might be helpful to know about the types of problems currently being solved using expert system techniques.

Below are classified the types of systems currently known about and in use. There are many ways in which one can categorise expert systems, but it is important not to get bogged down by classification.

| Type of system | Purpose |
|---|---|
| Interpretative | To infer situation descriptions from data |
| Diagnostic | To analyse system performance so as to highlight malfunctions of people, systems, or organisational performance |
| Design | To design objects given certain constraints |
| Planning | To propose courses of action under different scenarios |
| Monitoring | To compare and evaluate actual observation again plan |
| Education and training | To provide and transfer knowledge to students in an appropriate fashion |
| Control | To diagnose, debug, repair and monitor system behaviours |

To date most of the expert systems that have been developed have been by scientists for scientists. It is only now that they are being introduced as commercial applications aimed at solving business probems. The year 1987 promises to herald a rapid development of commercial applications.

The appendix to Chapter 8 includes a list of potential applications and Chapter 6 — Competitive Advantage through Expert Systems — as well as Chapter 8 — Identifying Meaningful Applications — will discuss in detail ideas of how management might meaningfully identify an application that might solve business problems.

## 2.3 INFORMATION TECHNOLOGY AND STRATEGIC DECIS-ION MAKING

Strategic decision making has a very wide impact on the direction and momentum of the organisation and aspects in the organisation which can be regarded as strategic are increasing and not decreasing. Any activity or function which has the potential to exert competitive 'leverage' in favour of the organisation needs to be considered in a strategic context.

Computer aids to decision making have mushroomed over the past 5 years. Spreadsheet programmes took off in popularity as managers came to grips with their ease of use and the ability to perform sensitivity analyses or 'what ifs' on different types of decisions or strategies.

Full blown decision support systems are the most recent information support system of managers. These are particularly popular for strategic planning purposes as they can, amongst other things, analyse trends, develop projections and evaluate the outcome of different courses of action against preset criteria. The new decision support tool that is being developed is the knowledge-based system. This will provide expert input into strategic decision-making tasks and is known as the expert system.

An appropriate information strategy is one where management leads the technology and not vice versa. By anticipating changes in the market and how the organisation intends responding to these changes, management is required to anticipate its information technology requirements, and to develop an appropriate investment and implementation programme that will meet those needs.

## 2.4 CURRENT DEVELOPMENTS

If you still have your doubts as to whether expert systems will pervade our workplaces and ultimately reach our homes, it might be sobering to have a brief review of what is being done.

It is said that Europe currently lags in the expert systems race by 12 to 18 months. The United States dominates the expert systems market at present. The market in the United States and Canada in 1986 was in excess of $300 million. By 1990 it is forecast to be in the order of $3.5 billion. Expert systems development in France, Germany and the UK is estimated to be $150 million during 1986 and estimated to be well in excess of $1 billion by 1990. The Japanese are deeply committed to AI and expert systems. As has been already mentioned, in 1982 they set up a ten-year research and development programme called the Institute for New Generation Computer Technology (ICOT). This is funded both by the Japanese Government and industry and has been dubbed the fifth generation project. The Japanese expect these new 'intelligent' machines to change their lives — and everyone else's. They believe the new wealth of nations will depend in the future upon information, knowledge and intelligence.

The greatest constraint recognised by those involved in expert systems development is the current lack of operational systems. So far most success has been achieved in the very high technology areas — but this is fast changing, as we shall see.

## 2.5   WHERE ARE WE GOING?

Post-World War II industrialised economies were essentially production economies. The 1950s and 1960s gave way to the fleets of salesmen with company cars, large expense accounts and large tummies. The production director was king until he was outranked by successful, high quota salesmen.

The 1970s saw the rise of the accountant, and to a far lesser extent the information technologist. The accountant started to dominate the organisation's proceedings. He held the purse-strings, implemented rigid capital budgeting proposal forms and developed a mania for taxation. The information technologist was no better understood or loved. However, his apparent ability to get dumb machines to perform repetitive, onerous tasks was reluctantly recognised.

The 1980s have fostered the organisational behaviourists and the management consultants. A consequence has been:

— the rise of the marketing man (as opposed to the salesman)
— the recognition that information technology has a strategic part to play and information technology is now getting board level representation
— a realisation that accountants should have a less significant role to play in the overall strategic affairs of the organisation
— a re-emphasis on people, culture, and corporate climate
— an awakening to the vital commodity of information and knowledge.

It is to be hoped that in the 1990s management will be able to integrate knowledge and experience in a positive and congruent way. The future is destined to bring technology even closer into our lives — no longer a blunt instrument but one that may be potentially sharper than we are.

## Current developments in technology

The Japanese 'fifth generation' project (commenced 1982)

This is a large-scale national research and development project directed at developing computer systems for the 1990s. These computers are intended to learn, associate, and make decisions similar to the way humans perform these tasks. The Japanese intend developing both hardware and software which will be conceptually and functionally different (refer KIPS). Intelligent interface machines are planned to replace the input–output devices of the fourth generation computer.

British 'Alvey' programme (commenced 1983)

This is a five-year programme aimed at improving the UK's competitive position in the world's IT markets. The technologies being focused on are:
— microelectronics
— software engineering
— intelligent computer based systems
— the human–computer interface

The European ESPRIT programme (commenced 1984)

The European Strategic Programme for Research and Development in Information Technologies (ESPRIT) is also a five-year programme. R & D continues into the areas mentioned under the Alvey programme as well as office systems and computer-integrated manufacture (CAD, CAM, robotics, etc).

# 3

# The importance of knowledge to the organisation

Among the key assets held by any organisation is the human knowledge, reasoning ability and expertise inherent within that group of people. The success of the organisation will lie largely in its ability to harness the individual abilities and expertise in a positive and meaningful way. The attitude of managers to their peers and other working staff is all important in creating an environment in which people can excel. By recognising that every member of staff, whether in the board-room, in the office or on the shopfloor can, and should be seen as a knowledge worker, managers are likely to stimulate confidence, loyalty and a sense of commitment. As was discussed in Chapter 1, people are motivated by being engaged in meaningful tasks; by gaining regular and timely feedback on their efforts and by feeling responsible for the results of their performance. A person who can utilise the full extent of his knowledge in the workplace and who can enhance that knowledge through wider exposure and increased experience, is likely to become an effective and dedicated employee.

## 3.1   KNOWLEDGE IS POWER

Is the statement that knowledge is power intuitively obvious, or does it need to be proven from first principles? Surely the more knowledge we have and can apply to a problem or situation the greater our ability to understand

— the boundaries
— the complexities

— the opportunities
— the relationships, and
— the causation of that problem or situation?

If the people in Country A have greater knowledge about the world, its politics and economics, and its socio and cultural variations they are likely to out-think and outperform Country B that possibly leads a more introverted and introspective life style. Similarly Organisation A that gears its workers to increasing and clarifying their own knowledge base will have a distinct advantage over Organisation B that expects workers to perform, rather than to think, apply knowledge and then perform.

Adam Smith (in his *Inquiry into the Nature and Causes of the Wealth of Nations 1776*) conceived of society as an energised circular flow of goods and money. The societal machine consisted of land, labour and capital which could grow and bring owners and nations wealth, political and economic power. The past 200 years has seen the more mature economies achieve some of that. The Less Developed as well as the Newly Industrialised Countries (NICs) are straining to imitate the perceived social, economic and political successes of the mature and maturing economies.

One could argue that another, even more successful commodity is required for national, organisational and personal success — that commodity being *knowledge*. This book supports the view that we are moving to a knowledge-based society; that we will develop knowledge banks as we have developed blood-banks, grain banks and money banks; that we will design knowledge bases at the same rate that we designed data-bases; and that the new form of arbitrage will be 'your knowledge versus mine'.

## 3.2   WHAT IS KNOWLEDGE?

Both knowledge and intelligence are highly abstract concepts. Although most of us have a fairly good idea of what they mean, and more especially how they relate to our own make-up, we have probably not explored some of their wider meaning in a universal context.

A dictionary will show that the verb 'to know' is used in a variety of ways. We can speak of knowing

— as an ability to recognise or identify something or someone
— as an ability to distinguish one thing from another
— as being acquainted with something, e.g. he sure knows his Shakespeare
— as the facility to recall facts, experiences, concepts and the like
— as being aware or apprised of something
— as having theoretical or practical understanding
— as having experienced something, e.g. I know what it is like to feel
   unprepared,

and so on.

Knowledge on the other hand is described as

— familiarity gained by experience
— a person's range of information;

and knowledgeable is commonly considered to be well-informed or intelligent.

Knowledge is continuously increased as a result of exposure to new perceptions, facts and situations imprinted in the mind and manipulated by reasoning ability. The more heightened the senses, the greater the exposure and the better the reasoning ability (often referred to as intelligence), the more astute the ability to accumulate and apply knowledge.

Reasoning ability is described as that ability to make inferences or deductions based on facts or given premises. An important point to remember is that either the facts or premise (or both) can be invalid and therefore our acquired knowledge need not necessarily be valid or true. Philosophers seek nothing else but to study wisdom and truth and thus to arrive at 'perfect' knowledge. Those who are not philosophers no doubt also seek perfect knowledge, and use their own methods to test the validity of facts, premises and our inferred knowledge thereof.

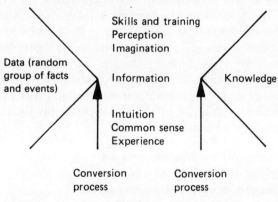

Fig. 3.1

The difference between knowledge and information is not always immediately obvious. Knowledge embraces a wider sphere than information. As set out in Fig. 3.1 knowledge includes not only information but skills and training, perception, imagination, intuition, common sense and experience. Knowledge is the sum result of our perceptive processes organised in such a way that significant conclusions can be drawn. Each individual has a personally derived rule base that organises his knowledge. It is the rule base of 'knowledgeable' experts that expert systems seek to capture.

The understanding of human knowledge demands far more rigorous discussion and scrutiny than that devoted to it in this text. Without in some way setting out the realms of knowledge we could hardly arrive at some agreement on how important it is. It is important in that it is the sum output of perceptive processes — vision, hearing, touch, smell, taste and thought.

For the purposes of this book and the objectives it sets out to achieve let us describe knowledge thus:

---

**Human knowledge is compiled experience**

- believed to he held in the human mind as heuristics
- it is apparently infinitely extensive
- it has redundant properties
- it includes heuristics about heuristics, about reasoning and onself
- it is incomplete, uncertain and inconsistent
- it can sometimes be inaccurate or plain wrong

---

### 3.3   EXPERT KNOWLEDGE

A question which is often posed is what is, and what makes for expert knowledge. I shall endeavour to address the former first.

Experts are those who have special skills or knowledge in (usually) a fairly narrow and definable area. In jargon this is referred to as the *domain* area. The expert can solve complex and unusual problems which the average person would be unable to tackle. Further, his problem-solving ability is likely to be more efficient and successful than the efforts of non-experts.

Other than the personal attributes of an expert, such as advanced skills gained as a result of practice or superior insight and intelligence, expert knowledge is enhanced by

— familiarity with the subject area
— attention to detail
— the opportunity to share knowledge
— a creative and open environment.

The expert demonstrates his expertise by being able to apply effective heuristics (rules of thumb) in order to solve his problems. These rules of thumb have become impressed in his mind and form part of his ('the expert's') knowledge-base. These rules enable him to screen information and to filter the alternatives in an incisive manner. As a result he can quickly grasp the kernel of the problem, and narrow down the range of potential solutions.

Part of the special skill of the expert is his ability to apply sequence, timing and the use of combinations to maximum effect in solving his problems.

One of the problems with human expertise is that it is often difficult to articulate. Experts are often not conscious of their decision-making processes or of the finely tuned heuristics that they apply to different problems. Acquiring this expertise is a problem area in the development of expert systems — this will be expanded upon in Chapters 10 and 11.

All organisations seek to have more experts which they can employ in gaining some form of competitive edge. Few organisations recognise that each member of staff has the potential of being an expert in his field — no matter how narrow the domain area!

## 3.4   THE KNOWLEDGE WORKER

A trite but very valid comment made is that an organisation or a group of people is only as strong or as effective as its *weakest* link. Weak could mean ineffective, disloyal, short-sighted, unintelligent or downright dumb. Natually the contributions made by individuals to the whole will vary, and that some contributions will be more effective than others is obvious. What leadership seeks to achieve is to motivate all contributors to perform the very best they can *relative* to *their* role in the pursuit of the organisation's objectives.

Every worker in an organisation has some knowledge of his role and function, and most have developed some expertise in that area. Be it the waiting-room attendant, the messenger, the chief engineer or the finance director, they all have some relevant knowledge. *Some* knowledge is less readily transportable than other knowledge — this is what makes some people's talents more expensive than others. Often, the most valuable knowledge, that of the organisation itself, goes unrecognised and unrewarded. What organisations and management often fail to recognise or grant scant recognition of is the importance of the knowledge of the organisation held by employees themselves. They are aware of, among other things, the formal and informal networks; they know how tasks are split up and allocated; they know who and what makes certain things happen and where weaknesses or bottlenecks may occur. This type of knowledge is invaluable to the organisation if suitably harnessed. The typist who has pounded out the organisation's stock sheets, invoices and letters; the switchboard operator who recognises the customers/clients by voice and name; the foreman who knows the production problems and bottlenecks like the back of his hand; the administration manager who has to keep the back office working optimally in the face of budget cuts and political infighting. This knowledge has as much strategic benefit to the organisation as that of, for example, brand management, pricing and financing techniques.

It is not only knowledge of concepts and techniques that is important. It is also the knowledge of people, facts and events that make up our experience and influence our perceptual ability. As organisations strive for an often miniscule competitive advantage, recognition of the knowledge-worker is bound to ensue. The 1990s herald the age of the knowledge-based society.

## 3.5   THE KNOWLEDGE-BASED SOCIETY

Jean Piaget, the world-famous Swiss psychologist, pointed out, amongst other things, that knowledge is a *process* rather than a *state*, i.e. it is constantly evolving. This has some very important implications. Firstly the pursuit or search for knowledge is a continuous, non-ending activity. No one, other than possibly the great sages, has reached a state of sublime knowledge — and even the sages once reaching nirvana in this world moved onto the next. Secondly, knowledge is improved by constant use. Once it no longer plays an active role it becomes redundant and ineffective. Thirdly, the knowledge which each individual has accumulated is unique to him. It has culminated as a result of personal skills, abilities, experience and intellect. It is something in which the individual normally has a certain amount of pride and wherein lies his identity. Fourthly, by searching for knowledge the *process* now assumes as much importance as the *result*. For westerners in particular, this is a new concept. The heady boom and bust days of the 1970s and 1980s have made them very results oriented. Many are inclined to seek the quick fix guide to results. This can no longer hold in a knowledge-based society where the seeking and recognition of knowledge is uppermost.

The emphasis on the process need in no way detract from the setting of the goals or the efficient attainment thereof. The Japanese bear ample testimony to this fact — and by no coincidence. They have openly declared their policies with regard to seeking wealth and economic success in the long term (goal definition), and by concentrating on specific processes which unite government and industry in collaborative efforts.

The move to a knowledge-based society should also hopefully remove some of the inequities in life. A society seeking quality (and aiming to diminish inequality) is likely to place greater emphasis on *what* you know rather than *who* you know. This movement will naturally be met with mixed response!

The wise men say
Do not seek to improve others —
strive to improve yourself.

## 3.6   KNOWLEDGE AND EXPERT SYSTEMS

Expert systems can offer a number of possibilities for greatly enhancing the assembly and use of knowledge.

We know that experience is the benefit of incremental hindsight. Imagine creating a knowledge-bank that could harness communal (corporate) hindsight? Imagine assimilating the knowledge of the organisation's knowledge — workers into a reasoning machine? Consider the motivating influence of gaining the collaboration of all knowledge–workers in seeking greater *mental* productivity? We all know the vulnerability of the organisation to its prize experts not to mention to the employees who have been with the organisation for years and understand what makes it a vibrant and dynamic system.

Human experts are

— expensive
— scarce
— busy
— inconsistent
— emotional
— mortal

These attributes are part of the creative, imaginative and fallible human being. They can be partly eliminated or neutralised by a thinking machine, which has as its heart the corpus of knowledge gained from the relevant experts of the organisation.

Expert systems are software programmes that experts can enrich with their knowledge. The systems can be built by one or a team of experts. The rule base can be altered by expansion or deletion and the rules themselves can be readily altered. Expert systems operate particularly well where the thinking is reasoning, and not calculating. They are designed to cope with uncertainty, which conventional systems are not. While in conventional systems the user interrogates the machine, in an expert system the machine is designed to question the user. Should the rule base either not have adequate rules to arrive at a solution or, the knowledge be insufficient or unclear, the system will alert the user. It will either request more information or it will indicate that due to the constraints imposed it can only recommend a less than perfect solution. The system offers the opportunity of fusing the knowledge of many experts so as to improve both the techniques and the results of problem solving. It also gives the organisation an opportunity of managing the knowledge in a dynamic way (see Chapter 4).

Expert systems provide the following opportunities:

• the incremental development of a (or many) knowledge base(s) over time;
• the knowledge base(s) can be in any identified, meaningful area of the organisation;
• the knowledge base can (and should) be modified on a continuous basis in line with the changes in knowledge, the environment and the organisation;
• the expert system can
    — suggest solutions to a problem
    — interrogate the user for more information

— explain its reasoning
— provide a record of both information received and conclusions reached
— amend its conclusions based on new or changed information.

In Chapter 1 we discussed the pursuits of modern management, and classified these under the building of corporate culture, the search for competitive advantage and the minimisation of cost of capital. It was highlighted that the right people, suitably motivated, are the key to organisational success.

Expert systems could be a unique tool for motivating the knowledge workers of the organisation. Potentially, all knowledge workers could participate in the development of knowledge banks. They would thus be obliged to place increased emphasis on their thinking processes. The *real* experts would emerge as people expected to contribute to the in-house knowledge arsenal of the organisation. The process of decision making would be challenged and talents existent but not normally used in the mainstream of organisational activity could be encapculated in *knowledge-able* decision making. By participating in analysing their own problem-solving processes people would be encouraged to deploy themselves better.

The communal effort to seek out, capture and transfer knowledge, promises the ingraining of a new corporate culture, a new look at quality and a spirit of autonomy and entrepreneurship.

# 4

# The role of knowledge in strategic decision making

Strategic decision making is one of the primary functions of management. In order to carry out this activity effectively, distinct goals need to have been set, the appropriate infrastructure needs to be in place and suitable resources should have been optimally allocated.

It is management's decision-making ability that will set the organisation apart from other organisations, and it is the process of making those decisions on which we will now focus.

## 4.1   THE DECISION-MAKING PROCESS AND DECISION SUPPORT

The decision-making process is fairly common to all individuals. As set out in Fig. 4.1 we

— are exposed to data
— reorder and analyse this data so as to have some form of information which tells us something meaningful;
— make further assumptions, predictions and inferences about this information so as to be able to focus on that information which is most relevant to the *decision*  and to the *criteria* associated with choosing that course of action.

For the most part, the analysing of information and the inferencing process is carried out at an unconscious level. As we are confronted with both so much information, and so many decisions to be made, a large

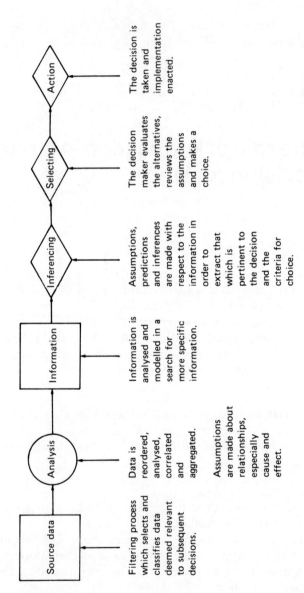

Fig. 4.1 The decision-making process.

portion of the decision-making process would appear to be automatic. Thinking processes are highly procedural, the more experience and knowledge, the more intuitive the process.

What makes our decision-making ability unique to each one of us is not the process *per se* but:

— the speed with which we handle data and information;
— the amount of relevant data we have to hand;
— the clarity and insightfulness with which we analyse, correlate and reorder the information;
— the discernment that we apply to the making of assumptions, predictions and inferences, and
— our cognitive style.

An effective decision maker is not only one who can respond in time with well thought out and clearly articulated decisions, but also one who is not afraid of making the decision and taking responsibility for the consequences! How often has it been said, 'No-one will take a decision around here!' or 'At least someone took a decision, even if it was the wrong one'?

The greatest concern of a decision maker is the consequences of either not taking an appropriate decision when it is required, or the taking of a decision that proves to be a wrong or bad one. The greater the strategic nature of the decision the wider the ramifications and the greater the impact of the decision — especially if it proves to be wrong.

## 4.2   COGNITIVE STYLE

Many factors affect decision making and the concept of *cognitive style* is an important one. The cognitive style of an individual is unique to him, in that it is the systematic and persuasive way in which he thinks.

Cognitive style is the manner in which an individual (1) perceives data and (2) formulates knowledge from the assimilated data. Naturally the type of information and the decision support tools required by a decision maker will be influenced by his cognitive style.

Cognitive style, training, experience and intelligence will together influence the effectiveness of the decision maker. There is no right or wrong style and the style employed will often vary according to the situation or circumstance.

With regard to *cognitive complexity*, however, it could be argued that the *greater* the complexity the more knowledgeable and effective the decision maker should be.

## 4.3   DECISION SUPPORT

In an increasingly complex world, decision makers strive to minimise the risk of being unprepared or making the wrong decision. The decision maker

| Category | Properties |
|---|---|
| *Cognitive complexity* | (1) differentiation — being the number of elements sought and assimilated in the cognitive process |
| | (2) discrimination — being the manner in which varying stimuli are assigned |
| | (3) integration — being the number and completeness of rules used in the cognitive process; |
| Field independence | This is the individual's ability to perceive patterns of data relatively independent of their context or as discreet items embedded in their context; |
| Thinking mode | This is the tendency to search data for causal relationships either in a systematic or heuristic manner. |

Fig. 4.2   Some categories of cognitive style.

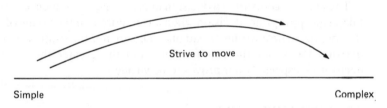

Strive to move

Simple                                                                      Complex

Fig. 4.3   Continuum of cognitive complexity.

thus seeks 'decision support' to assist him in coping with, *inter alia*

— many, complex decisions
— evaluating the risks of selecting the inappropriate decision
— the increased speed and urgency with which he is expected to respond
— a rapidly changing environment
— the pressures of changing environment
— the pressures of competition

Decision support is also required in order to provide psychological support.

The 1980s have seen information technology respond to the demand for more and better (more sophisticated) decision support. Decision support systems, usually providing algorithmic solutions, developed on fourth generation computers, have spawned a new industry of soft- and hardware consultants, eager to assist us in improving the quality of our decisions and aspiring to convert uncertainty (the unknown) into definable and measurable risk.

What is important to bear in mind is that any decision support tools:

● are only as good as the assumptions on which they are based;

- usually do not take cognisance of the qualitative issues which affect decisions. These issues are often the most important as they can have the widest ramifications;
- require to be well communicated to all those who are both directly and indirectly affected by their use;
- need to be maintained and reviewed on a regular basis if they are to maintain their relevance;
- should never become the scapegoat for management indecisiveness and/or political bickering.

Managers are essentially faced with three types of decision

— unstructured
— semi-structured
— structured

Usually, the more unstructured the decision the greater the number of unknowns and the more constrained the information available. This means that a fair amount of uncertainty exists in relation to the appropriateness and correctness of the decision. A tool that can assist the decision maker in coping with uncertainty is very welcome!

The manner in which an expert system handles uncertainty differs with different types of system as well as with the type of computer software used. Naturally, systems will need uncertainty to be highlighted in different ways. In some cases probabilities might be assigned while in others the areas of constraint are purely highlighted. For example, some expert systems have Bayesian probability analysis built into them. This means that a statement or conclusion can have a 'certainty factor' ascribed to it. e.g. There is a 65% chance that the economic scenario as described will result in an increase in interest rates.

Other types of systems can be designed to highlight the extent to which uncertainties exist. For example, if the knowledge included in the system is insufficient to arrive at a firm conclusion the system can point out the knowledge that is missing. It is important when designing and reviewing the performance of an expert system that all those concerned understand how the respective system copes with uncertainty.

An important point to bear continuously in mind is that both decision support systems and expert systems provide support to the decision maker and do not substitute for him. No form of system can absolve the decision maker from his responsibilities or replace human judgement.

The differences between decision support systems and expert systems have been set out in Fig. 4.5.

In summary:

Decision support systems
— are directed at essentially semi-structured decisions
— they endeavour to integrate the use of management science methods

| Type of decision | Important (Not urgent) [1] | Urgent (Not important) [2] | Important and urgent [3] | Neither — but have to be made [4] |
|---|---|---|---|---|
| Unstructured | Expert system | People-based as rarely are support tools available | Very senior staff plus Expert Systems plus DSS* | People-based — not economical to develop systems |
| Semi-structured | Expert System with DSS interface | Limited use of DSS | Extensive use of DSS | Very limited use of DSS |
| Structured | Senior staff | Simplistic DSS could be used if high volume of decisions | Senior staff | Junior staff |

Fig. 4.4   Types of decisions and decision support.

[1] Assuming significant commercial impact.
[2] Speed of decision making is the critical factor.
[3] These type of decisions must be the essence of the business and thus require as much support as possible.
[4] These are either few or irregular decisions with minimal commercial impact.
* DSS = Decision Support Systems.

| | DSS | ES |
| --- | --- | --- |
| Objective | Assist human | Replicate/mimic human behaviour |
| Decision maker | The human | The system |
| Major orientation | Decision making | Transfer of expertise |
| Query direction | Human queries the machine | Machine queries the human |
| Typical clients | Individual and/or group users | Individual user |
| Manipulation | Numerical | Symbolics |
| Problem area | Complex, integrated, wide | Narrow domain |
| Data-base | Factual knowledge | Procedural and factual knowledge |

Source: R. H. Sprague and H. J. Watson (eds), *Decision Support Systems, Putting Theory into Practice* (Prentice–Hall, 1986).

Fig. 4.5 Differences between Expert Systems (ES) and Decision Support Systems (DSS).

— they are flexible in providing support and not answers
— they can confront the problem in several different ways
Expert systems
— are problem-solving systems in a specialised problem domain area
— they attempt to mimic the thinking (skills and intuition) of the expert
— they use heuristic problem solving (rules of thumb) rather than optimisation techniques and formal reasoning
— suggest a solution to the problem.

The more unstructured the decision the greater the risk and therefore the more emphasis on and investment in support tools.

Expert Systems are an advanced form of decision support where the *cognitive* style of the expert whose knowledge makes up the knowledge-base can be analysed and evaluated. The strategic manager is faced continuously with complex and unstructured decisions, where there is a high level of uncertainty and a lot at stake. Previously, these situations were fairly infrequent and irregular — now they are the order of the day. The use of technology in playing a meaningful role is on the increase and the symbiotic development of 'man-and-machine' is the race to the future.

## 4.4 MANAGING KNOWLEDGE AS A STRATEGIC CORPORATE RESOURCE

Strategic decision making determines *where* the organisation is going and *how* it is going to get there. Strategy embraces direction, the extent of the effort and its timing. In order to carry this out astutely management requires:

— knowledge and understanding of the environment
— knowledge and understanding of the organisation's strengths and weaknesses
— knowledge and understanding of the customers
— knowledge and understanding of the organisation's competitors
— knowledge and understanding of employees and other resource attributes

Knowledge and understanding have been highlighted as the key input to a coherent and co-ordinated managerial strategy. The sum total of the relevant knowledge existing in the organisation needs to be recognised as a *major corporate resource*. Managing the knowledge base implies

— a search for completness (i.e. extending it as far as possible)
— fostering integration of the knowledge of different aspects of the organisation
— revising and updating the knowledge by collaborative questioning and testing amongst the domain experts.

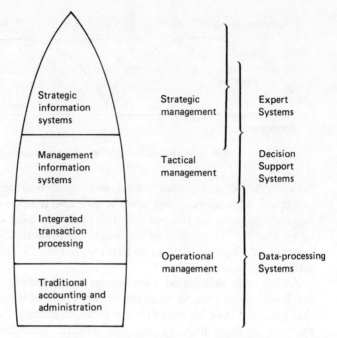

Fig. 4.6  Information technology and management.

Managers should encourage the development of knowledge banks by collecting the workers' knowledge on markets, customers, products, competitors, the use of resources, and so on. Yet again the Japanese have led the field here in *managing* the knowledge inherent in their workers by establishing Quality Control Circles as a method for managing parts of their business (elaborated on in Chapter 6).

*Knowledge banks* contain facts and rules about certain domain areas, e.g. competitor analyses, pricing strategies, capital budgeting, employment law, and so on. Knowledge banks need to be considered as live systems to be continuously modified and updated.

## 4.5  THE PROCESS VERSUS RESULTS-ORIENTED ORGANISATION

In the search for a short-cut to organisational achievement, too much emphasis has been placed on results, i.e. as long as you get there it does not matter how! Management is inclined to reward people for short-term results rather than longer-term achievements, looking for quick profits rather than lastring wealth.

Process-oriented people and organisations concern themselves with the methodology, the infrastructure, the stakeholders (as opposed to the shareholders), the resources and the future. Results-oriented people and organisations concern themselves with the present, or near present, with the rewards and with the exit options.

The process is part of the result but not vice versa! A healthy balance

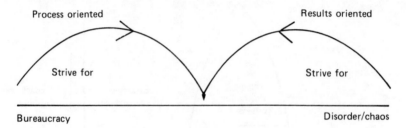

Fig. 4.7   Process versus results-oriented organisation.

between the two is required, as total bureaucracy is as ineffective as disorder and chaos. Management that sets the tone and tempo between a balanced emphasis on both the process and the result, will most certainly gain from better results. The tension or organisational pressures will be ameliorated and there will be time to promote harmony between stakeholders *en route* to profits, wealth and success.

As has been mentioned a knowledge-based society will place as much emphasis on the process as on the result. Think of the number of patients that have had their ills cured by sophisticated drugs only to be crippled for the rest of their lives by the side effects. True knowledge and due consideration of all the relevant facts and circumstances should diminish the use of panaceas.

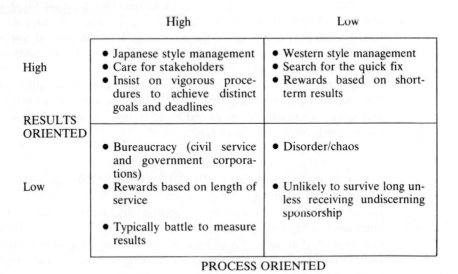

| | High | Low |
|---|---|---|
| **RESULTS ORIENTED** High | • Japanese style management<br>• Care for stakeholders<br>• Insist on vigorous proce-dures to achieve distinct goals and deadlines | • Western style management<br>• Search for the quick fix<br>• Rewards based on short-term results |
| Low | • Bureaucracy (civil service and government corpora-tions)<br>• Rewards based on length of service<br><br>• Typically battle to measure results | • Disorder/chaos<br><br>• Unlikely to survive long un-less receiving undiscerning sponsorship |

PROCESS ORIENTED

Fig. 4.8

# 5

# What are expert systems?

Human beings are always trying to find new things to do or new ways in which to do things. Artificial Intelligence and expert systems in particular, strive to fulfil both these aims simultaneously. As we move increasingly to a knowledge-based society (a concept which will be developed throughout this book) we continue to establish new mental and physical horizons. Since the beginning of time, man has used his reasoning and intellectual abilities to design and develop instruments to aid him in the challenge of daily survival. This pursuit continues at breakneck pace. In our relatively sophisticated society we now call these instruments machines; and the challenge of survival is known as establishing competitive advantage.

## 5.1   THE CONCEPT OF EXPERT SYSTEMS

Technology is part of daily life from the moment we turn off the alarm clock to the last moment at night when we set it. With the aid of machines we drive to work, prospect for oil, design aircraft, manipulate numbers, write letters and fly to the moon. Machine aids man in *carrying through* his actions, thoughts and ideas. Machines have yet to help man to think, or even further, to think for him. The revolution in computer technology proceeds unabated. It is to the computer that software scientists are looking to create an intelligent artefact to tackle intellectual tasks which would challenge a genius. For centuries scientists and philosophers have been preoccupied with man's ability to think — '*Cogito ergo sum*' (I think therefore I am) (René Descartes, *Discourse on Method* (Penguin Books, 1970).

This ability to *think* and *reason* sets man apart from the rest of the world. Man's thinking, other than day-dreaming, meditating or reflecting, is primarily engaged in problem-solving activities. It is this problem-solving ability that scientists wish to analyse and understand and then to harness in a 'thinking' machine.

---

**Artificial Intelligence** is that area of computer science concerned with making machines perform tasks which, were they performed by humans, would be considered as exhibiting intelligent behaviour.

**Expert systems** are a specialised form of Artificial Intelligence (AI). They are designed so as to replicate the problem-solving techniques of an expert in a narrow area of specialism, where reasoning is applied rather than calculation.

**Reasoning** is that ability to 'think out' or try to reach conclusions from valid or invalid premises.

---

Table 5.1.

## 5.2 THE CHALLENGE

The challenge of creating a reasoning machine stems essentially from:

— The problems of making an inanimate machine emulate the complex performance of a human being.
— Our inability to fully understand the processing mechanism and power of the human brain.

While computer scientists grapple with the hardware and software challenges, behavioural scientists continue to analyse and hypothesise how humans actually solve problems.

Our preoccupation with trying to understand how humans reason and thus solve problems is understandable. From morning to night our lives are filled with a series of decisions which have to be made:

What time should we get up?
Should we get up?
What should we eat?
How shall we dress?
What plans need to be made for today?
For the future?
How should be behave?
Where shall we meet to *decide* on our next course of action?

| Perceived advantages of a thinking machine | | |
| --- | --- | --- |
| *Characteristic* | *Human ability* | *Machine ability* |
| Knowledge | Perishable | Permanent |
| Reasoning | Inconsistent | Consistent |
| Expertise | Expensive | Affordable |
| People | Mobile | Immobile |
| Processing ability | Inconsistent | Consistently fast |
| Stamina | Limited | Unlimited |
| Expertise | Confined | Portable |
| Thinking | Mortal | Immortal |
| **Limitations of a thinking machine** | | |
| *Characteristic* | *Human ability* | *Machine ability* |
| Knowledge | Evolves (a process) | Static |
| Reasoning | Unlimited | Limited |
| Expertise | Adaptable | Rigid |
| People | Perceptive | Imperceptive |
| Processing ability | Multiple | Singular |
| Thinking | Conscious | Unconscious |
| Expertise | Creative | Uninspired |
| Common sense | Some | None |

Table 5.2.

and so on.

Even more interesting than analysing the *types* of decisions we make is understanding *how* we make them. What *knowledge* do we typically need to have so as to arrive at acceptable decisions? We need to bear in mind that decisions are based on judgement, and our judgement is influenced among other things by:

- the facts we have to hand
- past experience
- intuition
- gut feel
- perception (of various kinds)
- emotion, and
- common sense

Can we really computerise all these features of human problem solving?

## 5.3   HOW FAR HAVE WE GOT?

The concept of AI first started taking root during the 1950s.

Through the 1960s and 1970s great advances were made in developing computer-supported techniques which could emulate some of the natural capabilities of human beings.

Examples are speech recognition and synthesis, computer vision, robotics, understanding natural language, engaging in dialogue and different levels of problem solving.

The early AI efforts to develop problem-solving programs used search techniques rather than knowledge in order to simulate problem solving. Not only was this a highly inefficient method as the search could continue through an almost infinite number of alternatives, but the solutions could often be inappropriate or completely wrong. It soon became apparent that not only were general problem-solving programs not the answer but also that there existed insufficient understanding of how we generally think.

During the 1970s it became apparent to the AI scientists that a more selective approach was required in order to adequately solve real-world problems. Two specific breakthroughs stimulated the development of what is now termed *expert systems*.

The first was that problems are best solved by applying knowledge rather than trial-and-error search techniques. The second, which directly follows through from the first, is that the more narrowly and specifically the problem area is defined, the more powerfully the knowledge base can be applied. Thus began the development of rule-based systems that are able to reason about their own search effort as well as being able to propose a solution within the domain area.

Expert systems are thus 'intelligent' programmes that have encapsulated within their rule base the expertise (know-how) of a human expert. This expertise guides the computer in solving a problem or in arriving at a decision. The expert system will interact with the user by asking questions; explaining why it requires certain information; providing advice; justifying the opinion that it offers and explaining which conclusions it reached on the way as well as how these were arrived at. A fundamental requirement of expert systems is that they must contain knowledge (a concept that was explored in further detail in Chapter 3). Suffice it to say here, that knowledge is typically represented using rules, facts, heuristics and certain basic premises. One thing that expert systems cannot encompass, however, is *common sense*.

---

### Key characteristics of an expert system

- it is a sub-branch of AI
- the system manipulates symbols rather than numbers
- the system makes inferences and deductions from information provided to it
- *knowledge* is applied in order to solve the problem
- the problem area is narrow and specifically defined
- the knowledge base is used to guide and constrain the search for a solution (see combinatorial explosion)

---

The 1980s have seen an explosion of expert system projects. One of the reasons for this impetus has been the Japanese Fifth Generation Computer Project. To date most of the applications of expert systems have been in medicine and engineering, however commercial applications are rapidly appearing. The latter part of the 1980s is destined to herald one of the most intensive battles of our modern times — the fight for domination in the international market for commercial applications.

## 5.4   BUILDING AND EXPERT SYSTEM

Building an expert system is akin to any software engineering project in that it requires manpower, hardware and software, time and commitment.

### 5.4.1   Manpower requirements

Expert systems typically require a domain expert, a knowledge engineer and a potential user of the system.

The domain expert is a knowledgeable person who has gained a reputation for producing consistently better than average solutions to complex problems in a particular field. The expert (or in some cases, experts) applies his expert knowledge by developing rule bases that employ facts and heuristics to optimise the search for an acceptable solution. It is commonly recognised that experts are often unable to articulate their knowledge. Over time the expert's reasoning becomes increasing intuitive and embedded in his thought processes. Often the expert has limited self-awareness as to how his mind processes solutions — a fact particularly relevant to heuristic knowledge. In order to facilitate knowledge extraction a knowledge engineer is employed, who interviews experts and observes them at work in order to organise the knowledge and decide how it should be represented in the expert system.

The user is the person who will have potential use of the system. He should participate in specifying the *purpose* of the system, *who* the users are likely to be, and *how* the system should be used. Their role is invaluable in providing the feedback to developers as to the effectiveness of the evolving expert systems in addressing the ultimate audience.

### 5.4.2   Machine requirements

*Hardware*

There is many a debate as to whether expert systems can run as efficiently on microcomputers as they can on mainframes. As with most things the answer 'depends ... '. Obviously large, complex systems need larger hardware than smaller, less complex systems. At present expert systems are being run on all sizes of hardware. As expert systems usually require a lot of memory their development will naturally be inhibited by the hardware storage capacity.

An expert system usually consists of the basic components set out in Fig. 5.1.

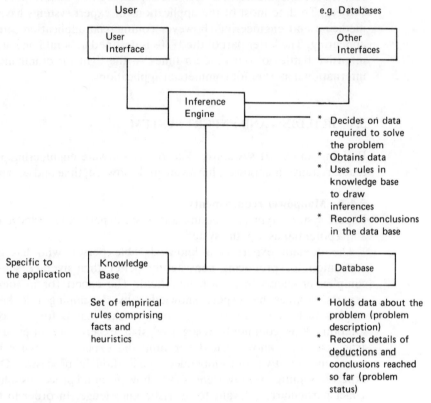

Fig. 5.1   Expert system software structure.

Simplistically:

- the inference engine drives the requests for data to solve the problem and applies the rules as encapsulated in the knowledge base
- it arrives at certain conclusions *en route* to solving the problem
- it interrogates the user for more information if and when required and is interrogated by the user with respect to any or all of:
  — why a particular question was asked?
  — what conclusions have been reached so far?
  — how were these reached?
  — which conclusions led to the proposed solution?

### 5.4.4   Time

Time requirements with regard to building expert systems are fairly substantial. There is insufficient experience to date, especially with regard to commercial systems, to provide any hard and fast rules on the investment in time. The importance of managing time will be discussed in greater detail in Part III — Getting Started.

### 5.4.5   Commitment

Commitment is that all important ingredient that is required in order to successfully carry through most things in life — equally so, if not more so in developing expert systems. These are new types of software engineering projects with new purposes, new opportunities and new problems. Like most things, you will only get out what you put in — and even that is not guaranteed!

### 5.4.6   Cost

Assessing the costs of developing an expert system, from start to finish, is similar to describing the length of a piece of string. The end cost will naturally depend on the purpose, size and complexity of the system. In any type of software development, especially where the software itself is in the development stages and the development of applications is not a common activity, the soft costs (i.e. people, incidental and opportunity costs) are usually high. In the case of expert systems, at this stage in their life cycle, this would most certainly be true. While the monetary implications of the different types of software tools are not discussed here, I think that trying to give some order of magnitude is probably in order. A small, fairly uncomplicated system, developed either as a prototype or as a mini-system using a user friendly shell will cost in the order of £25,000 to £60,000. For anything else more complex or integrated, the sky is the limit. The current mean cost of a full blown system developed on a mainframe, is held to be in the order of £750,000.

### 5.5   EXTRACTING, REPRESENTING AND UTILISING
###        KNOWLEDGE

*Handling* the knowledge is one of the most intricate parts of expert system development. The power and success of the system will depend on how ably this is carried out.

Expert systems development can be likened to the concept of 'putting the sea in a bucket'. Two very distinct problems are evident — which bucket to choose and then how to harness the sea, which, like knowledge, is infinite, unbounded and continuously changing.

The problems related to extracting knowledge and utilising knowledge will be discussed in Chapters 10 and 11 in greater detail.

### 5.5.1   Representing knowledge

Expert systems aim to replicate human reasoning power and processing techniques. The facts and rules are not always certain, accurate or true. Expert systems are designed to reason rather than to calculate and currently *most often* use *if–then* rules as representation. (There are other methods which will not be elaborated on here.)

The basic form:

*If* (condition)

*Then* (conclusion)
For example:
  *If* the application is meaningful
  *and* the expert is available
  *and* the knowledge engineer is sufficiently skilled
  *Then* consider building an expert system

## 5.6   THE PROBLEMS AND CONSTRAINTS

Expert systems are still in the fairly early stages of development. As yet there is insufficient collective and shared experience from which to espouse hard and fast rules on which to base the development and/or applications of expert systems. No methodology developed has yet been generally accepted.

The problems and constraints which one needs to be aware of are *inter alia*:

- the relative infancy of the technology
- the often unrealistically high expectations of the user community
- resistance to change
- the present paucity of commercially viable applications being implemented
- lack of knowledge engineering skills
- lack of integration between expert systems and conventional data processing systems
- the difficulty of determining of meaningful applications
- the problems with knowledge elicitation and self-ordained experts
- gaining commitment from both the *expert* and *senior management*.

There are other problems such as staff feeling threatened with respect to their jobs and the legal implications of expert systems. I shall endeavour to address all of these problems throughout the book. This does not mean that they will be eradicated — as *intelligent* human beings we need to reason out an acceptable solution suitable to *our* specific circumstances.

## 5.7   INFORMATION TECHNOLOGY AND STRATEGIC DECISION MAKING

The previous chapter 'The Role of Knowledge In Strategic Decision-making' discussed the importance of knowledge to the organisation as a strategic resource. It also highlighted the potential use of decision support systems, in a variety of forms, in order to utilise both information and technology to optimal advantage.

The biggest challenge facing organisations in the late 1980s and beyond lies in finding ways of harnessing information technology to serve business needs. Computers can no longer be relegated to the back-office. Data processing, telecommunication networks and the full spectrum of office computing services serve to make up the *strategic* grouping of information technology

systems which will have a profound effect on the success and profitability of
the organisation.

There is no question that the ability to respond to market challenges in a fast
and efficient manner is essential to organisational success. This chapter does
not seek to prove this fact, but rather to use it as a basic premise for the
discussion of the role of information technology in strategic decision making.
Information technology can assist the organisation in developing and
sustaining a competitive advantage by, for example, improving methods of
production, marketing, distribution, finance and administration. Information technology has and is likely to become the nexus of new methods in
developing differentiated products, creating barriers to entry and providing
interrelated and intelligent data-bases.

It has become the central support of any business and must be recognised as
a vital resource that requires to be managed as effectively as capital or labour.

## 5.8   INFORMATION TECHNOLOGY STRATEGY

Businesses are increasingly recognising the need for an information
technology strategy. This requirement is as a consequence of market changes
as much as being dictated by in-house IT architectural needs. Market effects
are increased competition, the requirement for *more relevant* information
and an environment of rapid and radical change. In-house technology
requirements are driven not only by increasing demands for information but
also the need to have integrated systems that can be developed into
distributed networks.

The evolution of information systems can be viewed as set out in Fig. 5.2.

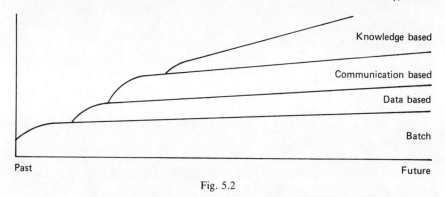

Fig. 5.2

Originally organisations used information technology for large batch
processing. Here the system performed large repetitive tasks, e.g. preparing
invoices off-line (usually after hours). This activity evolved into on-line,
interactive and distributed processing.

Stage 2 saw the development of data-bases in all parts of the organisation.
This development can be considered as the first major recognition that
information collected and accessible in a meaningful manner, could provide a

competitive edge. Communication-based systems have been the major thrust in the 1980s whereby systems are designed to communicate to one another and thus to make information collection and retrieval more powerful. The current stage of development in information technology is that of knowledge-based systems — and expert systems in particular. It is no coincidence that highly successful companies exploit information technology in developing their strategies, to the full.

# 6

# Competitive advantage through expert systems

This chapter discusses the leverage points at which competitive advantage can be gained and highlights the vital role of both knowledge and information. The notion has already been put forward that competitive advantage is the modern word for survival. We talk of survival of the fittest; the fittest being the one who can adapt to his environment and turn the problems and challenges to opportunities and advantages. In our turbulent and dynamic world we need to be fitter, more flexible and more informed in order to assure ourselves of surviving in the longer term. Personal fitness does not always transport itself into organisational fitness for reasons which management consultants have explored extensively. Organisations need to have strategies and plans in order to secure a wealth generating ability for all stakeholders in the longer term. They do not want barely to survive but to create and sustain an advantage over their competitors that will provide sufficient margin for errors and calamities as well as providing some quality of organisational life. No one wishes to be associated with the forever ailing organisation.

## 6.1   WHAT DOES IT MEAN TO GAIN COMPETITIVE ADVANTAGE?

The desire and drive to gain competitive advantage incites managers to do many things — some inspired and others possibly not so. But what does it really mean to gain competitive advantage? Gaining competitive advantage is getting better *relative returns* for the efforts of the organisation *vis-à-vis* the *known* and *identified* competitors who serve the *same* markets with a *similar* product or service.

Should an organisation not be able to outperform its competitors in at least some aspects of its activities it will ultimately be squeezed out of the market. Its sales and profits will decrease, it will no longer generate cash, it will lose customer credibility and market confidence. It will be bought out, stripped or simply wound up.


## 6.2   HOW TO CREATE A COMPETITIVE ADVANTAGE

We have established that organisations need to be better than the competitors in some facet of their business in order to participate in the sales potential of that market. Competitive advantage will be achieved once target market consumers start showing a preference for the organisation's offering over that of the competition. This preference can manifest itself in many ways, however it ultimately translates itself into more sales. Provided the costs of making the product or service are lower than the revenue therefrom this should be a happy state of affairs.

Table 6.1 puts forward the major ways in which an organisation could achieve competitive advantage.

The three key forms of competitive advantage are: a cost advantage; being able to differentiate the product or service offering through a range of techniques and/or being able to acquire or establish a strategic location from which to operate. The ways in which an organisation can establlish a competitive advantage under these three (non-mutually exclusive) headings is unique to that organisation's objectives, strengths and weaknesses and managerial potential. The manner in which an organisation will outperform its competitors will often change throughout the life cycle of the product, groups of products or the organisation itself. Competitive strategy can only be successful if it is appropriate to the environment prevailing at the time.


## 6.3   HOW TO SUSTAIN A COMPETITIVE ADVANTAGE

In many ways this is a more difficult challenge than initially creating an advantage. Most organisations come into existence as a result of an entrepreneur identifying an unexploited opportunity in the market. If this proves to be an accurate assessment, the organisation is likely to attract sufficient funds to prove itself during the usual three-year fledgling period. Having survived this critical time the organisation has had to probably expand its product base, penetrate new markets, serve new consumers and raise more capital. Daily survival depends on both creating new advantages as well as sustaining existing ones. As the rules of the competitive game are likely to change continuously it is important that management understands its business well and recognises the opportunities for optimising a cost, differentiation or location advantage. The more profitable the industry the

| *Forms of competitive advantage* | *Methods of achieving this — some examples* |
|---|---|
| • Cost advantage | |
| efficiency | Employee motivation, performance and control methods, sound planning and processes |
| technology | Modern technology for both the process and information accessing, processing and transmittal |
| processing skills | Efficient conversion of the generic product |
| resourcing skills | Better relative quality of materials, labour |
| marketing skills | Sound comprehension and anticipation of consumer needs |
| logistic skills | Effective, efficient and insightful scheduling of promises, processes and information |
| image (lower cost of capital) | Well articulated corporate marketing programmes |
| • Differentiation | |
| technology | Modern, innovative technology that differentiates the process, product, packaging, marketing, distribution or information content |
| quality/reliability | Usually relative to price and can be developed in any area of the organisation, e.g. resourcing, production, marketing and distribution |
| price | Relative to quality and consumer expectations |
| market understanding and awareness | Market research, use of interrelated data-bases and attention to customer service details |
| creation of barriers to entry | Use of special technology, cost advantages as a result of volume |
| information | Better access, deployment and transmission of relevant *information* and knowledge throughout the organisation |
| image/promotion | Suitable promotional campaigns, product packaging and image portrayal |
| • Location | High community congruence and convenience through profoundly placed distribution, marketing, retailing and information outlets. |

Table 6.1  Methods of achieving competitive advantage.

greater the rivalry not only between existing competitors but the likelihood of new entrants. The organisation needs to identify any areas in which it has, or is likely to have relative superiority, and to use that power point both as a defensive move in creating barriers to entry, as well as a platform from which to launch strategic offensive initiatives.

## 6.4   THE CRITICAL SUCCESS FACTOR (CSF) CONCEPT

The CSF concept is both a well known and thoroughly tried and tested one. Every business has certain factors which can be deemed critical to its success. CSFs are those areas that must be given special and continual attention by management as they also represent those critical leverage points that can be used to strategic advantage.

---

A *critical success factor* (CSF) is an aspect/activity of the organisation, the management of which is vital to organisational success

A *critical failure factor* (CFF) is an aspect/activity of the organisation, the poor management of which is likely to precipitate organisational failure

By definition a CSF is a CFF; however, a CFF is not necessarily a CSF.

---

Table 6.2.

The CSF method is often used to direct an organisation's efforts in developing strategic plans. Not only can it be a very effective method in focusing on the essence of the business in developing a set of strategies but it can act as a vital aid in identifying critical *information* that is required in order to implement those strategies.

---

*Some examples of CSFs and CFFs*

- Small high street jeweller
  - CSF location
  - CFF high shrinkage
- Health authorities
  - CSF quality/standard of service
  - CFF poor co-ordination of sub-contract staff
- Shipbuilding
  - CSF meet contract date
  - CFF trade union pressure
- Distributor of important equipment
  - CSF relationship with supplier
  - CFF foreign exchange

---

Table 6.3.

A consistent and coherent competitive strategy that embraces strategic thinking in a forward-looking manner, will only result if management:

— understands the CSFs and CFFs of the organisation
— uses this understanding to gain competitive advantage by either altering the cost structure, developing differentiation strategies or capitalising on locational factors
— uses information and information technology to maximum effective use

as we shall now see.

## 6.5  INFORMATION, INFORMATION TECHNOLOGY AND COMPETITIVE ADVANTAGE

Most organisations seek to make profits or minimise costs. *Profit* is a function of *price*, *volume* and *cost*. The way to make *more* profits is somehow to improve (or optimise) the relationship between these three factors. In order to do this the organisation needs to know:

— how well it is doing (internal information)
— how well others are doing (external information)
— what it could, or should do in order to do better. (internal and external information)

The organisation is thus vitally dependent on information in its endeavour to be both more effective and more efficient (Fig. 6.1). Being effective is the ability to attain the prescribed objectives and goals, while being efficient is the ability to achieve these with minimum effort. Effective organisations are most likely to be efficient but not necessarily vice versa. The necessity to be

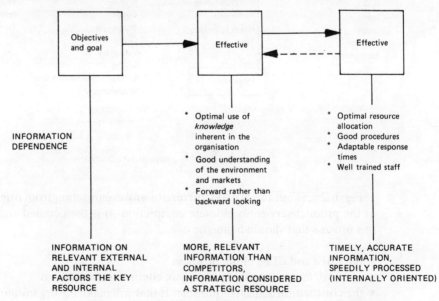

Fig. 6.1  Organisational performance and the role of information.

both effective and efficient has never been as great as it is today. The ability of the organisation to acquire and use information in *all* of its activities is destined to pre-empt its success or failure. Information and information technology is transforming the nature of competition and providing opportunities to create new forms of competitive advantage. Organisations will be able to use it to manage their CSFs by changing cost structures, developing new differentiation strategies and manipulating locational strategies (e.g. retail distribution networks). The use of information technology will alter the business economics of both individual businesses and industries. Investment into information technology research and development, hardware and software will continue to soar and raise the fixed cost levels of most organisations. While this will affect break-even volume levels, making firms dependent on greater volumes, use of information within the entire product offering will create added value and should improve the marginal contribution per product sale.

Whatever the organisational emphasis; production, distribution or marketing, clever use of information technology will provide a new path to creating and sustaining competitive advantage.

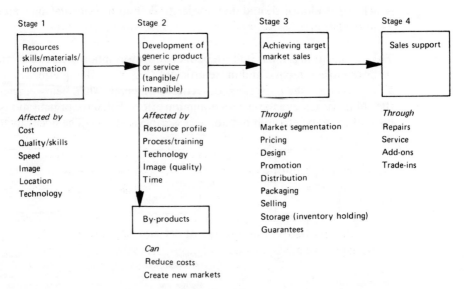

Fig. 6.2 Gaining competitive advantage.

Fig. 6.2 sets out the broad structure of any organisation from origination of the product/service to ultimate completion. It is the detailed analysis of this process that should highlight

- the CSFs and CFFs of the business
- points of leverage to be used to gain competitive advantage
- the critical information requirements that will make the organisation both more effective and more efficient.

Different industries are more or less information dependent. For example, industries that provide financial services, e.g. banks and insurance companies, are toally dependent on information in order to create, market, and distribute their products. As Walter Wriston, ex-Chairman of Citicorp, remarked some time ago, 'knowledge about money is as important as money itself'. In short, knowledge is traded rather than money.

The intensity of both information technology and process technology is increasing in all types of industry. There is a trend towards expanding the information content in products as well as using information technology to enhance distribution techniques. Note the publishing trade that is almost totally dependent on information technology to provide information to customers, to schedule and process orders, to manage inventories and to facilitate all types of sales support. The retail industry is highly dependent on sales throughput per square foot of sales area. This can only be achieved by sophisticated distribution support, sales analysis integrated with inventory analysis and other environmental factors such as, for example, weather, fashion and consumer spending trends.

By carefully reviewing the process of product origination to realisation and sale, management needs to identify at which stage competitive advantage could be developed. The role of both process and information technology can be significant. The greater the *knowledge* of the production, marketing and distribution processes and where their CSFs could be, the greater the possibility of dissecting the component parts and refining these to some distinct organisational advantage.

Gaining competitive advantage depends upon making good decisions. So whatever assists in making better decisions contributes to establishing a competitive edge. We have already explored the role of knowledge in strategic decision making (Chapter 4) and have highlighted some of the information requirements on which the organisation critically depends. Deciding *which* information is relevant, is as important as deciding *how much* is required, *when* it is required and *what*, if anything should be done with it.

This in itself is a series of decision-making processes. It is the recognition of this that has led to the upsurge of decision support tools, data support tools, data-base management, and more recently expert systems.

Let us take a look again at the decision-making process (Fig. 6.3). It is immediately obvious how information technology can play a key role in this activity.

## 6.6   COMPETITIVE ADVANTAGE THROUGH EXPERT SYSTEMS

Figure 6.3 highlights one key message, namely, expert systems is the only tool available at present that can actually propose a decision from a range of alternatives.

The selection process (i.e. the actual taking of the decision) is the major management function and assigned to managers because of the ramifications of taking decisions. By employing the knowledge worker who is the

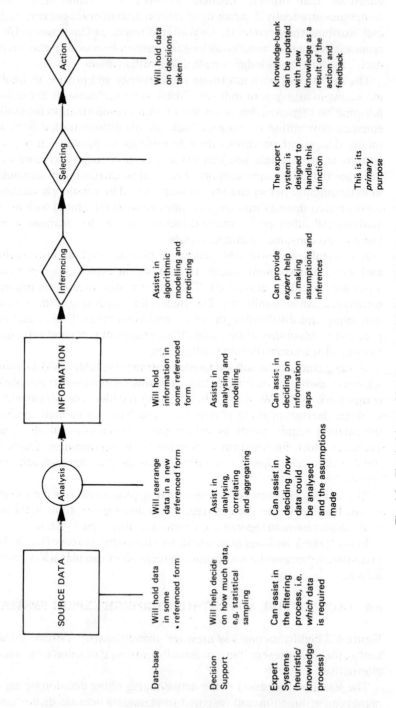

Fig. 6.3   The decision-making process and information technology.

*expert* in his domain to develop this system, *expert* decisions should necessarily follow, and need no longer be considered the preserve of management alone. The strategic implications of this are obvious. Using domain experts to solve organisational problems at every level, is one of the powerful strategies employed by the Japanese especially in their Quality Control Circle movement.

## 6.7   EXPERT SYSTEMS — AN EXTENSION OF QUALITY CONTROL CIRCLES?

Quality Control Circles (QCC) have been in vogue in Japan for the past decade. A QCC typically consists of from five to seven employees who work in a particular sector of the organisation, e.g. a part of the production line, who meet informally (normally during working hours) in order to discuss problems and opportunities related to their work. Staff are invited to share their knowledge and expertise so as to solve common problems in an efficient and unique way. QCC members can not only suggest changes based on their in depth analysis, but once management has some comprehension of what they intend achieving, and the manner in which they intend going about this, the staff are encouraged to implement their own action plans.

QCCs have received much acclaim from Western managements, especially those in manufacturing industries. It is argued that the effectiveness of QCCs in adding to the competitive advantage of Japanese industries could be replicated by organisations in other countries. This movement has already begun, e.g. Jaguar. It can be reasonably argued that applying expert systems in business is an extension of the Quality Control Circle movement.

# 7

# The impact of technological innovation—the human and social dimension

## 7.1   THE IMPACT OF TECHNOLOGICAL INNOVATION

The impact of technology on man and his environment is worthy of several volumes in its own right. This very brief chapter can only bring out some salient points which need to be considered. What history has shown is that technology wins in the end. Despite the Luddites, the need for the artisan and craftsman is all but over. The machine has penetrated every aspect of our lives. In the face of fairly strong resistance to automation, especially in some European countries, machines are not only performing *more* tasks but design engineers, with the aid of computers, are designing increasingly specialised and sophisticated equipment. Tasks that were originally considered to be the preserve of man are now being executed with greater precision and skill by machines. If this is evidence of progress the critical question is — is progress a good thing?

There has been and continues to be a vociferous debate as to whether the concentration of power is laudable. The industrial revolution is often criticised for its supposed 'detribalisation' of the masses forcing them to relinquish an agrarian economy and to move to an industrial and mechanistic society. It is argued by some that man is viewed only as an economic workhorse who should fall in with society's need for high relative productivity and performance.

In general, people do not want to be automated. They wish to involve themselves with new technology — yes — but in their own time and at their own pace. They need to feel that they are in control and not that a legion of robots is waiting in the wings ready to advance and to dominate. Managing the rapid advancement of technology is part and parcel of the management of change. As Machiavelli so aptly pointed out, change is most difficult for those who aim to bring it about.

The impact of technology will naturally affect different groups of people differently. Where its use heightens the feeling of stature and self-worth it will be well received and exploited to the full. Where this is not necessarily the case, technological advancement will be viewed with suspicion, distrust and even hatred.

## 7.2   MAN VERSUS MACHINE

Man's quest for meaning is as old and as long as the history of man itself. There would appear to be two forms of meaning which man seeks to experience. The first is that of self-meaning. This is the need to have a feeling of self-worth, of dignity and self-importance. The desire for self-meaning is normally very strong. For some it is a torturous road. It does not always bring out the best in one, often the contrary is true. Victor Frankl in his well known book *Man's Will to Meaning*, explores man's will and desire for self-meaning. Many of his thoughts crystallised during his own traumatic imprisonment in Auschwitz during the Second World War. As a psychiatrist, he pondered upon why some people survived certain (devastating) circumstances while others did not. The second (related) form of meaning is that of significance. Relative to his own socio-group man wishes to be recognised and at least remembered with some distinction.

The human value system, in many ways individual to each person, is inextricably bound up with the need for self-meaning and recognition. Self-meaning provides purpose, and recognition brings acceptance and responsibility. Man is essentially ego. His perception of the environment and his view of the future is enormously influenced by how these impact his view of himself. Science has dealt several blows to man's ego. Galileo, Darwin and Einstein, amongst many, have put forward some very convincing theories about man in his universal context. He is by no means master of the universe but only part of it. What makes him distinctive, however, is his ability to reason and to think. How real will the blow to his endemic ego be if he now has to interact with a thinking machine?

Let us look at some of the positive and negative arguments that can be advanced with regard to technological innovation.

### 7.2.1   Positive arguments
- Technology can increase communication and thus co-operation.
- It can improve productivity.
- If man is free from more menial tasks he will have more time to be creative, reflective, cogitative and imaginative. He will be freed of tasks that are tedious and uninspiring and have more time to devote to meaningful activities.

- Technology enhances consistent quality.
- The advances of technology have generated new freedom for the sick, the aged, the disabled, the psychologically and physiologically disadvantaged.
- As a result of technology the world is that much smaller and intertwined and peoples and cultures are brought together.
- Technology advances our understanding of man. Psychological research has helped us understand how and why he functions, his thought processes and his perceptive ability.
- A major area of human endeavour, that of education, has benefited greatly from advances in technology. Intelligent computer-aided instruction is destined to be the norm for the future.
- People will be able to demonstrate their IQ in far more appropriate forms as greater emphasis will be placed on the abilities of both the left and the right side of the brain as computer technology evolves further to include both creative and analytical uses.
- By working smarter as a result of technological innovation, new and different jobs will be created.

### 7.2.2   Negative arguments

- Machines will become more important to socio-economic society than humans.
- People will become dehumanised (whatever that means) and be expected to function like machines.
- A highly mechanised society increases the paranoia of the less skilled or unskilled worker who sees the machine as taking over his job.
- As (most) people identify with their job not only for their own self-esteem but also with regard to how they are seen in the eyes of their peers, they need to feel positive about it. If the machine is now going to dictate the element of status applicable to jobs, this might denigrate the perceived status of the job in the eyes of the worker.
- As was discussed in Chapter 2 motivation is enhanced where work is meaningful, regular feedback is given to the individual, and the individual has a sense of responsibility for the outcome of his efforts. It can be clearly argued that technology can inhibit or even block any potential motivational forces as it often removes these opportunities from the worker. Some good examples of this are the manufacturing production line and the printing trade. In the past, workers in some of these areas were considered to be highly skilled craftsmen — this is no longer so. Technology has all but taken over the human skill that was originally required. These people must now consider themselves deskilled as they perform comparatively menial tasks subordinate to the mighty machine.
- Technology and automation, it is postulated, will concentrate even more power in the hands of the few. The clever and the rich will become even more elitist and Joe Average will sink further into relative insignificance.
- It is all very well to say that new and different jobs will be created — but where and by whom? What if they are not created? Despite millions of people being out of work, this is one area of society where togetherness

does not bring acceptance. The stigma attached to unemployment remains. No one wishes to be out of a job.

• Some argue that modern technology is still fairly crude. The man–machine interface is still considered to be harsh and unfriendly and those who shun computers say that they (the computers) are designed for the technologist and not for the man in the street.

• George Orwell's book *1984* described a mechanistic society where man was subordinate to the machine. Technology was used for man's benefit as ordained by the elite class who designed, programmed and manipulated them. 1984 has come and gone and technological advancement continues apace — many would argue to the disbenefit of mankind, for example: the development of nuclear plants, the Star Wars programme. These could be viewed as irresponsible progress.

• Some say that we will degenerate into a 'robotic' society where over-mechanisation and rationalisation of processes will denigrate the importance of human values. As a consequence we will think and respond like machines. Interpersonal relationships will deteriorate and generally the quality of life will diminish.

## 7.3   WHAT ABOUT THE CHILDREN?

When weighing the pros and cons of the increasing role of techology in our society let us consider for a moment the children. After all is it not for their benefit that we wish to take a stand. Is it not the quality of their lives that we wish to secure now?

For a child, some thirty years ago, the most advanced technology that he was exposed to was a pedal go-cart and possibly a kite. He probably used to play ball and house-house. What are children exposed to today? Remote controlled television, computer games and make-it-yourself videos are some fairly common children's pastimes. Even the most menial of workers has his dinner prepared by microwave oven while he settles in for the viewing on TV (or his rented video set). With the compliments of the never-never pay back scheme (the availability of instant credit for long periods of time) it would seem that in general we wish to experience the advantages of new technology but are unprepared to tolerate its disadvantages.

## 7.4   ARTIFICIAL INTELLIGENCE (AI) AND EXPERT SYSTEMS (ES)

Distrust of technological innovation, where it exists, is likely to be heightened by the introduction of AI and ES. As mentioned earlier, the resistance to the basic idea that a machine can not only think but may in the future be able to out-think man will, in some quarters, be very severe. The very idea will be regarded as preposterous and refuted even by those who are normally in favour of technical advancement. Let us look at some of the positive and negative sides to expert systems.

### 7.4.1   Positive aspects

- Expert systems can improve motivation and a feeling of self-worth, a consequence of which will be an improvement in culture (corporate and otherwise).
- There will be a new respect for people, not only as people but as knowledge workers.
- Expert system development will give recognition to the true experts and not the pseudo-experts.
- The harnessing and combining of expertise inter-culture and intra-culture could lead to a better world.
- New knowledge will be discovered more quickly and effectively as the computer discovers new relationships and combinations.
- New forms of expertise will be discovered and shared as the reasoning process encapsulated in expert systems can include artistic and logical reasoning.
- The cost of accessing expertise will decrease dramatically.
- We will learn more about our own problem-solving processes which will assist us in improving and vitalising them.
- Everyone (in theory) will have access to the same level of expertise, a cogent argument possibly for the medical field.
- Expert systems make us focus on knowledge as the road to self-improvement and excellence.

### 7.4.2   Negative aspects

- Expert systems will lead to undue emphasis being placed on *objective* knowledge. This could lead to a dehumanising view of man, as not all of man's knowledge can, or indeed should be expressed objectively. There may also be an inclination to undervalue the affective aspects of man. There may thus be a move towards recognising only those who are articulate and highly rational.
- Expert systems might lead to an increasing bias towards labelling people — expert, non-expert, articulate, inarticulate, and so on. As the world famous psychologist Carl Rogers has so often stressed, labelling people is exceedingly deplorable. Not only do humans have many facets to their nature, their make-up is unique to them and should be recognised. Mutual concern and caring for fellow man can only exist if we exhibit unconditional positive regard for one another — which precludes us from labelling one another.
- Computer knowledge may begin substituting for real knowledge thus making people feel inadequate about their own abilities.
- A serious threat posed by the introduction of expert systems is to those who cannot demonstrate any distinctive expertise. What will become of them? Will their bosses be computers?
- Another negative viewpoint could be the assignment of responsibility. Will the expert system have legal rights in the case of proposing an

incorrect solution? Can it be sued for professional negligence?
- Developing the expert system will deskill the expert. He might feel at risk once he has parted with his knowledge. He may have less value to the organisation.
- The potential threat of AI and ES is that it will diminish our quality of life as we perform less and less thinking for ourselves.
- People might get a distorted view of man who is supposedly essentially spirit and all that follows from that belief.


## 7.5   SOME CONCLUSIONS

There is no way that this book can resolve some of the very real and profound debates that surround the potential positives and negatives of technological advancement. Suffice it to say that they exist and are very necessary if we are to take a firm hand in guiding progress in a positive direction.

Views about the social and cultural implications fall into two distinct camps. There is the very positive view (recognising problems and constraints) and the very negative view that holds that little, if any good will result from AI and ES. Naturally there are more or less radical views within these two camps. There is no question but that this book seeks to present a tendentious view with regard to the former slant. It intends doing so in a sober rather than a superficial or extremist manner. The transitional phase, which we are now experiencing, is always the most traumatic. It is during this phase that the extremes of either position are often most exaggerated. There is no doubt but that every advance has its cost. The world is a world of trade-offs. It must be remembered at all times that:

- Expert systems are *not* a substitute for human judgement
- They can only apply to relatively small domain areas
- They need to be considered as live systems that need amendment and maintenance
- They can never include common sense, intuition or emotion
- They are designed by *real* thinking, feeling human people and are thus not perfect.

The author believes very strongly in the resilience, ingenuity and adaptiveness of people. Therein lies their greatest strength. Not only do people adapt but they do so very quickly and often with far less trauma and upheaval than predicted.

Leaders and managers have a responsibility to facilitate change. They need to recognise the opportunities and problems in an *informed*, *practical* and, where possible *objective*, fashion. Problems are not there to be ignored but to be addressed. The challenge of change lies not in recognising that it exists but in managing it to the betterment of our future and that of our children.

### 7.5.1   What response does AI and ES deserve?
- Learn more about it
- Prepare for it (positive as well as negative aspects)
- Educate those who are likely to be affected

# Part II

## The Strategic Applications of Expert Systems

# 8

# Identifying meaningful applications

There is no question that at this point in time the greatest challenge facing expert system developers is that of developing *meaningful* applications. Meaningful in this context has a far-reaching embrace. It needs to be above all meaningful to the organisation, its objectives and its strategies; it needs to be meaningful to the expert(s) so that he/they feel that they are not being taken up with trivia; it requires substance so that the knowledge engineer can perform a meaningful task, and it needs to be suitable for expert systems technology. Experience to date has shown that the choice of application is a fundamental contributor to either failure or success. This chapter provides a methodology for identifying applications that are likely to contribute to success.

The strategic implications of expert systems, as set out in Part I provided some ideas on what management sets out to achieve and the ways in which it goes about trying to do this. It is the intention to build on these ideas (especially Chapters 2 and 6) in order to develop the proposed methodology. As a consequence of the present shortage of successfully implemented commercial applications it is difficult to prescribe a yardstick for both costs and timescales appropriate to different types of system developments. As always, management is required to be suitably informed and to demonstrate sound common sense. Chapter 15 expands on the Stages of Expert System Development which includes further guidelines with respect to project management.

## 8.1   SUITABILITY

As was pointed out in Chapter 4, expert systems lend themselves to unstructured and semi-structured types of decisions. They are especially useful if the type of decision is important (i.e. it usually has a significant commercial impact) or both important and urgent. A meaningful application is thus one where the expert system can replicate the human behaviour of an expert in an important activity of the organisation where the expertise can be used or transferred.

## 8.2   The motivation behind expert systems development

- To disseminate expertise throughout the organisation, e.g. a system on selling techniques for a firm of consultants.
- To free experts for activities which demand their specialist skills. Here systems could be developed to handle the more routine problem-solving tasks so that experts could be freed up to handle the more creative and complex tasks. A good example is that of tax experts who are often taken up with fairly routine problem solving that could easily be encapsulated in an expert system.
- To provide expert education and training across a wide spectrum, which if it were dependent on the human expert, would never be attained due to physical and location restrictions. An example here might be the training of new employees in organisational safety or security procedures, where the organisation has many branches nationwide and only one or two safety/security officers.
- To provide surrogate experts in those areas where experts are in short supply or required only infrequently, e.g. experts on employment law or pension fund complexities.
- To provide a standardised or methodological approach to solving important, fairly unstructured tasks that require expertise. These are usually tasks that are not only complex in the number of alternatives that may need to be considered, but that the solution lies in a profile (or pattern) of conforming or non-conforming criteria. For example the whole question of capital investment appraisal might be a suitable example here (see the appendix at the end of Chapter 9).
- To develop a knowledge bank of explicit knowledge inherent in members of the organisation. This could compromise knowledge gained from in-house experts or from experts during their exit-interviews when leaving the organisation, e.g. equipment fault diagnosis or purchasing management techniques.

    Knowledge banks could also be developed not only for rare-skills archiving, but to broaden the knowledge in a particular area. Domain experts could combine their expertise so as to provide a wider perspective of an area, e.g. building a knowledge bank on consumer buying habits.
- To reduce equipment costs and/or speed up equipment dismantling or assembly. This type of system usually occurs where the expert system is the front end of a network of systems, often being AI systems, e.g. robotics.

- To explain statutory regulations or complaince procedures. This is particularly suitable if an organisation depends greatly on its employee being conversant with these, e.g. accountants, solicitors, liquidators, etc.
- To provide consistent and high quality evaluation and monitoring, e.g. equipment monitoring. Humans lose concentration and become fatigued whereas machines do not.
- To provide interfaces to complex systems. This is one area where expert systems are still very much in the developmental stages, e.g. natural language interfaces to databases.
- To design systems that assist decision makers in managing complexity. This type of system would not only propose a methodology or a procedure but could suggest areas where other functions or interfaces overlap.
- To develop a competitive edge by either improving the cost structure, reducing costs or developing some form of production, marketing or distribution differentiation. Using expert systems to achieve a competitive advantage is potentially the most exciting side to commercial developments. It is in this area that we are likely to see fierce developmental activity in the coming years.

Expert systems can be used to assist organisations in being more *effective* and/or more *efficient*. In order to make this a reality it is essential that management understands what it can expect from an expert system development and therefore approaches it with healthy restraint and realism.

Before launching into the details of a methodology let us remind ourselves what expert systems are and what their primary purpose should be.

---

**Expert Systems** are computer programs significantly composed of an explicit representation of human knowledge provided by one or more relevant experts.

This know-how is expressed as a series of facts and rules usually held in the expert's brain as heuristics.

The prime purpose of an expert system is to enable know-how to be exploited by those who are not experts.

The program needs to be continuously refined by relevant experts so that it minimises the redundancy of the knowledge.

---

It is not possible to provide iron-clad rules for determining whether an application is suitable for implementation as an expert system. Some guidelines are set out below.

### Positive indicators for using expert system techniques

- When rules of thumb are the most effective and efficient ways in which to arrive at a solution as the searching of all the potential alternatives could result in combinatorial explosion.
- When conventional techniques appear to be inappropriate or inadequate.

- Where the system can be used to teach as well as to advise.
- Where problems are solved by the application of rules rather than the use of equations.
- Where the system's knowledge has to be maintained by experts in the relevant area, rather than by computer staff.
- Where explanations of the system's performance are required, e.g. why a particular bit of advice was given, what conclusions have been reached along the way, and so on.
- Where a common form of expertise is required by many and only few proficient experts can supply it.
- Where the domain area can be clearly specified in that it is narrow rather than broad, and deep rather than superficial.

### Negative indicators for using expert system techniques

- When the potential application does not require know-how in order to perform problem solving.
- When knowledge about the problem is more readily available in algorithmic form.
- When the problem can be adequately and efficiently solved using conventional techniques.
- When the domain area is superficial or difficult to specify.
- When the decision process is highly structured and problem solving is simple and easily delegated.

### The overriding requirements for practical expert systems are:

- They must perform well (i.e. at least as well as a real, live expert) on complex problems; they must not give silly answers, even to silly questions.
- They must be implementable in that the domain is both narrow and specified, as well as being wide enough to be useful and meaningful without providing facile advice.
- The system must be designed in such a way that it is considered to be user friendly. The system must thus converse in terms that the user can understand.
- An expert system must be able to explain how it reached its conclusion. The knowledge base must be comprehensible when interrogated and should be able to explain why it needs certain information in order to arrive at conclusions.
- A system needs to be fairly easily modifiable without incurring a great deal of time or development cost.
- The running time of a system needs to be at an acceptable speed. No user will sit in front of an uninspiring monitor waiting for questions to be asked of him (the user), or for pearls of wisdom to be poured forth, if the time delay is unacceptable.

## 8.3   FEASIBILITY

The constraints on expert system development will be addressed in Chapter 13, and the role of the expert and the knowledge engineer will be discussed in Chapters 10 and 11, respectively. In principle an expert system development will be feasible if

— the task does not require imagination or common sense
— experts can articulate their methods
— genuine experts are available and co-operative
— the task requires cognitive skills
— the nature of the task is clearly understood
— the problem solving required is not too easy and is considered to be a serious one.

The importance of defining the problem as well as the careful structuring required will be addressed in the chapter on enlisting the expert and putting him to work.

## 8.4   VIABILITY

Establishing the viability of an expert system application is difficult. A full blown expert system application takes a relatively long time to develop, and the exact payoff is not always clear or even measurable after the event. Establishing criteria for (a) giving the project the go-ahead and (b) measuring its performance thereafter is no easy task. Chapter 9 seeks to provide some ideas on how to motivate an expert system proposal, what type of criteria might be used, and how to measure these if at all.

## 8.5   SELECTING A FIRST APPLICATION

As with all software applications the first one is in many ways the most important. The psychological effect of a success or a failure is normally enormous, mainly due to the habit of reaching too many conclusions about the technology from that one experience. Thus, some organisations have not prepared themselves adequately, or have chosen the wrong application which failed, and have then concluded that expert systems are impractical or unsuitable for them. This is a pity. Every organisation is full of potential expert systems or know-how applications. All projects carry a risk especially the first one — and this needs to be taken on board in advance. The extent of the risk can be minimised by

— being adequately prepared
— establishing clear objectives as to what the benefits of the system are expected to be

— having realistic expectations
— selecting an application that is relatively uncomplicated and clear cut
— confining the first project especially to a very narrow domain
— recruiting a suitable application team.

The selection of the application team for the first application is as delicate and as important as deciding on the first application. They should be enthusiastic volunteers who have been reasonably exposed to the concept of expert systems. They should preferably have some experience of working with computers and should thus not feel inhibited by new technology. The team should include an expert who is *articulate* albeit that he is not the most expert in the area of application. The team should include a knowledge engineer and possibly a programmer.

Although the team will be naturally inclined to broadcast its aspirations and progress, it may be advisable to temper this until real advancement can be openly demonstrated. Enthusiasm, however, is usually infectious and that type of breeding ground is likely to generate positive results. The most sensible objective for the first program is to get an experiential understanding of what expert systems really entail.

Suitable project steps will be discussed in Part III in getting organised.


## 8.6. IDENTIFYING APPLICATIONS FOR COMPETITIVE ADVANTAGE

We have discussed how organisations strive to be both more effective and more efficient; in Chapter 6 the information dependence of an organisation was highlighted. Effective organisations aim to be more knowledgeable about their environment, their competitors, their markets, their customers and their employees. Efficient organisations seek to use this knowledge to improve their operating, marketing, distribution and overall information processing abilities. Expert systems can potentially help organisations to be both more effective and more efficient. The greatest return will be gained by developing a knowledge base that can in some way help to manage or optimise the CSFs and possibly to monitor the CFFs of the business.

Particularly in experimenting with the first expert system application it is advisable to select an area that will improve efficiency rather than effectiveness. The motivation for saying this is that if the application does not work out or proves to be a flop, the worst that can happen is that the organisation is likely to be no more inefficient than it was before, and therefore nothing major will have been lost. If, however, the proposed application is in some way 'tampering' with or 'fine tuning' things like strategy, a poor result could have far more serious consequences.

A further consideration that may help in identifying a meaningful application is where the greatest leverage could be achieved. This is usually done by performing something new or different, or, improving on what has hitherto been done in the past.

| EFFECTIVENESS | * Setting the appropriate goals/objectives<br>* Good decision-making abilities (decisiveness)<br>* Knowledgeable about environment/markets<br>  customers/resources<br>* Ability to work smartly<br>* Employ the right people (skills and attitude)<br>* Ability to be adaptable and flexible<br>* Sound understanding of mechanisms<br>  — *when* best to use |
| EFFICIENCY | * Sound understanding of mechanisms<br>  — *how* best to use<br>* Lower relative cost than industry/competitors<br>* Better resource in/resource out ratio, i.e.<br>  optional resource allocation<br>* Sound methods and procedures (well understood<br>  and communicated throughout organisation)<br>* Employee motivation<br>* Flexibility as a result of comprehension<br>* Fast assimilation of information into the organisation |

Fig. 8.1   Methods of achieving effectiveness and efficiency.

Figure 8.1 outlines some activities that lead to effectiveness and some that lead to efficiency; every aspect outlined could be a potential know-how program for the organisation. What management is required to do is, starting with the first, least risky type of application, to select an area that would lend itself to a knowledge-based program based on the criteria set out earlier in this chapter. Another way of looking at an organisation's strengths and weaknesses as well as leverage opportunities is to view them as *internal factors* and *external factors*. Internal factors are those that relate to the internal mechanisms of the organisation (i.e. its internal environment); for example:

— quality control standards
— employee motivation
— internal procedures
— management information systems

While external factors relate to activities that interface with the environment outside of the organisation; for example:

— market or product differentiation
— knowledge of consumer behaviour
— market image (promotional strategies)
— impact on the environment, e.g. pollution controls


In identifying meaningful applications it is obviously important to decide on what can be described as *meaningful*. To have meaning could probably be described as having a significant purpose. Many managers would say that the only thing meaningful to the organisation is that which influences the bottom line (i.e. profits). Relative return on profits is often described as the *payoff*.

In looking for *payoffs* as a result of investment decisions, management needs to decide what their *payoff* expectations are — which may be one or a combination of several payoffs; Among others


- the highest payoff
- the fastest payoff
- the safest payoff (i.e. lowest risk)
- the incidental payoff (this project is incidental to something larger and more significant and therefore any payoff is an incidental, marginal benefit)
- the unmeasurable payoff — being something highly qualitative, subjective and difficult to measure, yet its effects are abundantly and forcibly evident
- no payoff — other than having experienced the experience (so to speak) — which is a payoff in itself.


Part of the criteria for identifying a meaningful application is thus finding one that has a *significant* payoff with *acceptable* risks. The concepts of significant and acceptable are highly complex and subjective and thus vulnerable to heavy debate. As always strength of personalities, politics and history will come into play — advice on which cannot be presented here. The important point that needs to be highlighted is that the perceived payoff is a very important and very subjective issue.

Further, it is a very emotional one in that a high payoff is perceived to be a glamorous one and (most often) vice versa. People like to be associated with a *glamorous* payoff albeit more risky, i.e. it has not only a greater chance of failure but the impact of the failure is that much more substantial. Often the payoff might be purely in the experience of developing a knowledge bank, and/or of combining and motivating experts in a common drive toward increased organisational effectiveness and/or efficiency.

The secret in identifying a meaningful application lies in having both a healthy motivation and realistic expectation of what can and cannot be achieved.

---

**Right approach**

**A blunt rule**
*If* expert systems technology *is* suitable
*and* meaningful application *is* identified
*and* expert system development *is* justified
*and* suitable expert *is* available
*then* consider expert system development

---

**Wrong approaches**

I have heard about expert systems. I am interested and would like to use this technology. Which application would justify my involvement with expert systems?

Expert systems are the 'in' thing. This is where I, as manager, can make my mark. Which is the highest and fastest payoff application that can be identified so that I can pull this off ahead of everyone else?

---

Above all — developing the expert system needs to be a rewarding and fun process even if the payoff(s) are not immediately visible, measurable or fully recognised.


## 8.7   RETURN ON INVESTMENT

Until expert system developments become more commonplace and an industry *knowledge base* on expert systems is established the return on investment (RoI) is difficult to establish.

The RoI most often enunciated with respect to expert systems is that

— there will be an increase in expert productivity
— there will be an improvement in expert capability
— expertise will be preserved
— expertise can be efficiently disseminated
— projects will be tackled that could not normally be tackled using conventional systems technology

Let us refer to Fig. 8.2 on gaining competitive advantage. Every organisation trades on what it believes to be its distinctive competence. In order to create and sustain this distinctive competence it needs to home in on

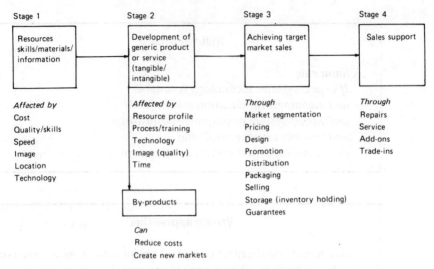

Fig. 8.2   Gaining competitive advantage.

those factors critical to making up that competence (the CSFs). The distinctive competence of the organisation may be one, but more often it is a combination of factors. Emphasis of upgrading performance in these areas is all important.

Further, the issues that impact these areas are likely to

— be deemed to be strategic issues
— have the greatest and widest impact on the rest of the organisation
— have the potentially highest and fastest payoff
— have the highest risk if the organisation were to neglect these issues or to take some bad decisions.

The best way in which to set out how an organisation might identify appropriate applications is to provide some examples. (The appendix to this chapter provides some further ideas with respect to expert systems projects.)

### Example 1

| | |
|---|---|
| *Type of organisation* | Accountants, financial and management consultants |
| *Perceived distinctive competence* | The ability to provide comprehensive advice on a wide range of issues and still maintain personal, caring contact with clients |
| *Target market* | Small to medium sized organisation |
| *Critical success factors* | Good recruitment procedures Training of staff on matters both internal and external to the organisation |

|                                            |                                              |
|--------------------------------------------|----------------------------------------------|
|                                            | Time                                         |
|                                            | Packaging                                    |
|                                            | Image                                        |
| *Critical failure factors*                 | Resource allocation                          |
|                                            | Market segmentation                          |

*Potential ES applications* (some ideas)

Recruitment

(1) An ES on recruitment procedures

(2) A knowledge bank on all skills of staff, even those which they do not use in their present jobs

(3) An expert system to match job profiles with candidate profiles

(4) An expert system advising on career planning and manpower resource requirements

Training

(1) An ES on staff regulations and compliance procedures

(2) An ES on quality standards to be applied to different tasks

(3) An ES providing advice on the application of statutory regulations

Competitor analysis

A knowledge bank on what is offered, by whom and where — and where gaps might be identified

Resource allocation

Expert systems or knowledge bases for resource allocation would tie in well with those on recruitment, e.g. an ES on optimal allocation of staff based on *all* their relevant skills

*Example 2*

*Type of organisation*

Financial institution — commercial and retail banking

*Perceived distinctive competence*

The ability to provide a total range of services to customers through a wide and comprehensive distribution network

*Target market*

Every man in the street and most types of organisations (size and location are irrelevant)

*Critical success factors*

Use and deployment of technology
efficiency
distribution
packaging

| *Critical failure factors* | pricing |
| | risk evaluation |

*Potential ES applications*
Expert systems in finance is a fertile ground for applications aimed at achieving some form of competitive advantage.

The pillars of finance rest on knowledge and information. It is clearly one of the most information intense businesses, and technology is a most strategic resource. The current development of commercial applications is evolving rapidly.

The appendix includes a list of potential applications wherein those in the financial field feature quite eminently. One of the areas most extensively investigated at present is that of risk management.

### Example 3

| *Type of organisation* | Retail store with national network |
| *Perceived distinctive competence* | The ability to provide a vast range of retail goods with better than average quality and highly competitive prices |
| *Target market* | The man in the street |
| *Critical success factors* | Location |
| | Sources of supply (materials purchasing management) |
| | Use and deployment of technology |
| | Width and depth of range (inventory management) |
| *Critical failure factors* | Evaluation of trends in consumer behaviour |

*Potential ES applications* (some ideas)

(1) An ES that can recommend sources of supply under certain given constraints
(2) A system that provides advice on in-store management to management trainees
(3) An ES interface for the decision support tools that recommend inventory holding volumes and mixes. This could propose optimal solutions and explain the rationale.

All of the examples cited are organisations that are very dependent on information technology. Then again there are not many that are not. Although only a few examples have been mentioned here possibilities abound. It would be to management's advantage to establish a think tank in order to consider possible applications. The secret lies in identifying those *knowledgeable* activities of the organisation that contribute to organisational success.

## 8.8  PROPOSED METHODOLOGY

***Proposed methodology — a path for management***
  (1)  Review the CSFs of the business and all related and contributory factors;
  (2)  Describe and evaluate the role of knowledge and information in creating and sustaining those CSFs;
  (3)  List all tasks/activities that contribute to establishing and sustaining the distinctive competence of the organisation;
  (4)  Of those items listed under (3) identify which contribute most to efficiency or to effectiveness and rank the potential payoffs that extra leverage could provide;
  (5)  Review whether any of these areas would lend themselves to an expert system application by reviewing criteria proposed at the beginning of this chapter;
  (6)  Rank the potential areas of application favoured for an ES application in some form of priority (see Chapter 9);
  (7)  Establish whether there are articulate, available and co-operative experts;
  (8)  In co-operation with the expert establish objectives, milestones and methods for measuring whether the objectives have been achieved;
  (9)  Evaluate the available tools that are likely to be suitable for the application and note the constraints that they might pose on the development;
  (10)  Appoint the application team and in due time formalise the brief.
(Refer Chapter 15 — 'Stages of Expert System Development and Project Management'.)

---

**Managers Wealth Warning**

  (1)  Expert systems — their application and implementation — must be the consequence of a sound, well researched *business* decision.
  (2)  The organisation should be apprised of what expert systems are, how the organisation might benefit and how employees might be involved. Memos from the chief executive will not do. There is nothing to beat a well prepared, well organised internal roadshow.
  (3)  Expert systems are purely a new (possibly more powerful and exciting) form of software technology. They must be treated as such.

Comprehension minimises apprehension!

---

## APPENDIX: POTENTIAL APPLICATIONS

### Strategy and policy
- Market strategy
  — the planning of strategy under different scenarios.
- Management consultancy
  — rare skills archiving.
  — art of negotiating: the system stimulates a negotiating session, plus guides in framing a strategy.
  — range of diagnostic tools that analyse business situations

### Management control
- System selection evaluation
- Scheduling methods and systems
- Estimating manufacturing costs
- Monitoring of performance
- Installation consultancy (of systems, procedures and equipment)
- Distribution methods and systems
- Optimising manufacturing techniques

### Industry
- Equipment control
- Decision support to for example
  — capital investment appraisal
  — expansion plans
  — make-or-buy decisions
- Operational activities
  equipment fault diagnosis
  materials handling methods and techniques
  design alternatives
  in-store management aids

### Insurance
- Evaluating risks
- Assessing claims
- Underwriting
- Broking

### Banking and finance
- Regulation based systems
- Corporate evaluation and credit assessment
- Risk evaluation
- Advisory systems
  — advice on finance required
       "   " credit analysis
       "   " investment management
       "   " arbitrage opportunities

" " take-overs and mergers
" " accounting procedures
- Optimisation of hedging strategies
- Portfolio management
- Assisting in treasury operations
- Foreign exchange exposure management
- Management of Letter of Credit

### Office automation
- Records management
  — expert assistance in mapping out policies and procedures
  — training the user in applying the procedures
- Message distribution
  — establishing priorities of the dissemination of messages
- Information retrieval
  — assistance in defining information needs and accessing suitable sources

### General business
  — A system providing income tax and/or tax planning advice
  — Financial analysis beyond the intelligent spreadsheet level
  — Data protection requirements
  — Statutory sick pay regulations
  — Employment law regulations

### Training programmes
This could take an infinite number of forms. Some examples might include:

— designing of tutorial sessions on any range of topics.
— in-house aids to getting to know the procedures of an organisation.

The book *A Guide to Expert Systems* by Donald A. Waterman (Addison–Wesley, 1986) includes a detailed list of the better known expert systems currently in use across a range of subject areas.

Information requirements are critical inputs to any stage of the organisational process, as is highlighted in the table below. (Refer to Fig. 8.2).

| Aspect | Information requirements |
| --- | --- |
| **Stage One: Resources** (skills/materials/information) | |
| Cost | How high/low? |
| | What do competitors pay? |
| | What could influence this? |
| Quality/skills | How is it measured? |
| | How is it acquired? |
| | What are the benefits? |
| | What is the industry norm? |
| | What are competitors doing? |

| | |
|---|---|
| Speed | How rapidly can suitable resources be acquired? |
| | What will affect this? |
| | How can the organisation improve on this? |
| Image | What does image mean in this context? |
| | How can it be developed and sustained? |
| | What image do competitors incorporate? |
| Location | Which is the best location? |
| | What criteria are used to decide? |
| | What is the rest of the industry doing? |
| Technology | What type and structure of telecommunications required? |
| | What type and structure of procurement technology available? |
| | What type and structure of warehousing technology available? |
| | What are the industry ordering and scheduling norms and delays? |
| | What type of technology used by competitors? |

| Aspect | Information requirements |
|---|---|
| *Stage Two: Development of generic product or service* | |
| Process/training | The process available? |
| | Use of technology? |
| | Competitor processes? |
| | Industry norms? |
| | Financing implications? |
| Technology | Latest technology available? |
| | Criteria for choice of appropriate technology? |
| | Comparative cost? |
| | Development potential? |
| Image | What does image mean in this context? |
| | How can it be developed and sustained? |
| | What are the cost implications? |
| | What image do competitors project? |

| Time | How long does the process take? |
| | How long do competitors take? |
| | Can the time process be improved on and, if so, how? |
| *By-products* | Can the yield be improved? |
| | Can the levels of cost be diminished? |
| | How best can these be marketed? |
| | How can new markets be exploited? |
| | What do competitors do? |

| *Aspect* | *Information requirements* |

*Stage Three: Achieving target market sales*

| Pricing | Should this be high, medium or low? |
| | How could pricing be improved? |
| | How do competitors price? |
| | Can discounts, credit and deferred sales improve customer perception of the price? |
| | What is the industry norm? |
| | Are goods/services price elastic? |
| Design | What is a suitable cost-effective design? |
| | What are the criteria for choice? |
| | What are competitors doing? |
| | How can technology assist, e.g. CAD/CAM? |
| | What does the target market appreciate? |
| Promotion | What could be considered to be a cost-effective promotion campaign? |
| | What are the criteria for measurement? |
| | What are the competitors doing? |
| | How are target markets responding? |
| | Which is the most cost-effective media? |
| Distribution | What are the most cost effective distribution channels for the product? |
| | What do the competitors use? |
| | What do customers appear to prefer? |

|  | How can technology aid distribution? |
|  | Does distribution add value? If so, how? |
| Packaging | What is the most attractive form of packaging? |
|  | How could this be made to be cost-effective? |
|  | How do competitors package their products? |
|  | Do customers purchase the product for its package, e.g. attractive jam-jars? |
|  | How can technology improve the package? |
|  | What type of information is required on the package? |
| Storage | How can the organisation store its product or service? |
|  | Should it hold stock or sell to order? |
|  | What service levels do customers expect? |
|  | What is the cost of holding inventory? |
| Guarantees | What type of guarantees are considered to be the industry norm? |
|  | What do customers expect? |
|  | What do competitors offer? |
|  | How can these be used to strategic advantage? |

*Stage Four: Sales support*

|  | What is considered to be sales support? |
|  | What are the costs thereof? |
|  | What do competitors offer? |
|  | What types of information are required in order to offer effective support? |
|  | How can technology help? |

The above analysis provides some idea of the enormous amount of information on which the organisation depends. Formerly management did not take enough time to understand how information sensitive a business is.

This is changing rapidly. The awareness is very much heightened and the guidance that management now requires is related to the best ways in which they can acquire, store, reorganise, manipulate and transmit, information.

# 9

# Motivating the proposal for an Expert System development — the investment decision

Throughout this book implications and applications of expert systems have been discussed in a managerial context: it is the distinct objective throughout to bring the idea of this technology closer to the manager. We have discussed the strategic decision-making process and the issues surrounding competitive advantage in some depth. Part and parcel of the issues focused on by management is that of the investment decision; long and hard debate exists as to whether *raising* the finance deserves more emphasis than *investing* that finance. This particular view can be strongly contested, and a strong argument put forward:

(a) that there is no shortage of funds;
(b) rather that there is a distinct shortage of sound (backable) projects;
(c) and that a well researched investment proposal that can demonstrate at least average market returns will be able to attract the required finance.

It is in part (c) of the above argument that the greatest problem often exists for the seeker of funds. The complexities inherent in the development of investment proposals are well known. The potential borrower very often feels that he has a sound, well researched proposal, and his biggest problem, or so he believes, is convincing the potential lenders or investors. For a start-up organisation, management buyout team or organisation requiring substantial refinancing, interaction with lenders or investors can be a tedious and complicated affair. Often the nexus of the business is subject to critical scrutiny and its prospects are evaluated from first principles. An organisation that is not in the throes of restructuring, refinancing or the like, should have or should have access to, a source of funds that enables it to sustain healthy trading activities. Healthy, in this context, means consistently profitable.

Management's resistance to ES developments most often lies in the apparent difficulty of presenting an investment proposal that promises an acceptable monetary return. As most managers are faced with more projects than funds, those with better financial prospects tend to get funding approval more readily.

Deciding to embark on an expert system development should be viewed as a specific long-term investment decision. To a greater or lesser extent, depending on the project envisaged, it should be subject to some of the rigours normally facing investment decisions. Often investments in software or hardware are left to the relevant technologists to research, plan and propose to those who have the authority to grant sanction. In the case of an expert system development this should most certainly not occur. A cross-functional group of people should be involved as the useful deployment of expert systems has the potential to affect a very wide range of functions throughout the organisation: Chapter 14 — Preparing the Organisation for Expert Systems — will discuss the optimal manner in which to involve suitable people.

## 9.1   THE INVESTMENT DECISION

Investment decisions in organisations usually fall under the heading of capital *budgeting*, as all organisations have a finite source of funds which they can use for their investments. These capital funds, need to be invested in those projects which are likely to generate the greatest benefit to the organisation in the future; benefit being measured as a maximisation of profit or a minimisation of cost. The key element of a capital investment decision is the commitment of resources now in return for some anticipated gain in the future. This gain is normally spread out over several years, the first year being in itself some years hence from when the decision was taken. Management thus takes a decision with regard to the allocation of its resources so that, in some way, some time in the future they (the resources), will have either improved or increased. An important part of the capital budgeting process is not just the allocation of money capital but also that of human capital.

Improving the qualities and capabilities of human capital means making them more knowledgeable, more adaptable and more skilful. A more capable workforce is likely to utilise more of its skills in performing its tasks, improved human capital is usually a forerunner to greater monetary capital. As has been propounded throughout this book — the investment in expert systems has the potential for intensifying the qualities and powers of the organisation's human capital.

Capital investment decisions are complex as:

— they commit resources for a long period of time, usually several years
— the quantity and quality of the returns are not guaranteed, to the contrary, they are usually highly uncertain
— the timing of the returns is not certain
— the amounts involved are usually substantial
— there are usually several projects or needs of the business competing for funds making project selection difficult
— the criteria for deciding on the justification for the investment is often subjective, arbitrary and open to misinterpretation and/or dispute
— the true risks attached to the investment decision are not only often difficult to identify but in some cases they can be almost impossible to measure.

In a nutshell the problems facing management when it comes to investment appraisal is that the risks are high and the returns are relatively uncertain. The greater the amount involved and the longer the period of time taken up in the investment decision, the greater the risk and therefore the greater the return required in order to make the project appear to be a viable one. Managers who are measured and rewarded on short-term results are reluctant to forsake today's rewards in the hopes of something better in the future.

The benefits or returns required as a consequence of investments are usually translated into pecuniary gain. This is measured in the form of the net present value of future cash flows. This is calculated, based on the future cash in-and-out flows attached to the project discounted at some discount rate adjusted for time, inflation and risk. The benefits accruing to capital investment projects cannot all be measured in this way. Benefits and gains might not be immediately translatable into cash flow terms. The conversion process might be far more subtle and less easily identifiable as to cause and effect.

### 9.1.1  The risks related to investment decisions

A brief word on risk will surely not go amiss. The greatest risk perceived as adversely affecting investment decisions is that of time. In our fast-moving, fast-changing world, the further out in time that we contemplate and plan something, the greater the uncertainty the plan coming to fruition occurring in the pattern that origianlly anticipated. Risks are increased by the nature of the project, e.g. the number of people or functions involved, the likely impact on those people/functions (e.g. redundancy, changes in work groups, changes in location or operating methods, etc.); the financing methods employed and the expectations expressed by both management and shareholders.

## 9.2   EXPERT SYSTEMS AND THE INVESTMENT RISKS

Investments in information technology have proved to be a bitter experience for some. It would be fair to say that computer software developments in particular are considered to be fairly high risk for their commensurate returns. This is often as much a fault of management who do not involve themselves sufficiently in the proposal, as it is of those who are responsible for project delivery. Expert systems fall quite clearly into the category of software technology development, and are thus by definition considered a high-risk investment proposal. The expectations of management (i.e. the objectives set) and the difficulties in setting (a) the investment criteria, and (b) the acceptable bench-marks with regards to returns, do not operate in favour of expert system developments.

Added to this are several risks which, when combined, position expert systems in the *ultra* high-risk bracket. These are:

- the infancy of the technology
- the lack of commercial projects with which to compare or use as a precedent in establishing milestones during the developmental phase
- the highly qualitative and subjective side to the expert system application
- the difficulty, if not impossibility, in planning *incremental* cash flows as a consequence of the use of these new systems.

It is a truism to say that the higher the risk the higher the expected return. Sometimes those returns take a longer time to manifest themselves than one would naturally like. Attaining above average or exemplary returns requires taking calculated risks combined with a large dose of foresight.

## 9.3   THE MOTIVATION FOR AND CLASSIFICATION OF
##       INVESTMENT PROJECTS

A multitude of motivations exist which could culminate in a capital investment decision. Some of these are for offensive reasons while others are for defensive purposes, some are in order to improve effectiveness, while others seek to promote efficiency. Depending upon the type of organisation, the style of management and the dependence on technology, the response to long-term capital investment project will differ.

Investment in technology has seen an upward surge this decade, as has been already pointed out at length. Investment decisions in this area should be commonplace to most organisations and methods for coping with uncertainty will have been devised.

In order to establish suitable criteria for investment decisions it is helpful to classify these into categories. By reference to Fig. 9.1 investment decisions have been divided into revenue earning and non-revenue earning ones.

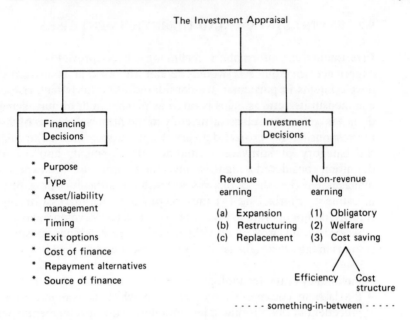

Fig. 9.1   Capital budgeting.

*The non-revenue earnings ones include*:

(1) **Obligatory** — this type of expenditure is usually required in order to comply with statutory requirements, safety controls, insurance contracts and the like. The important point is that this expenditure *must* be incurred to enable the business to continue. There is unlikely to be a great deal of flexibility over the timing of the expenditure. The investment criteria is likely to be based on the lowest cost alternative.

(2) **Welfare** — this form of investment is supportive to the business's main activities rather than being an integral part thereof. Examples would be office canteens, company cars and sports facilities for employees. The benefits arising from this form of expenditure are very difficult to predict or to measure. The anticipated returns are essentially highly qualitative. This is often the first category of expenditure to receive the axe if funds available for investment become severely limited. The investment criteria are normally highly subjective with the emphasis again being on the least cost alternative.

(3) **Cost-saving** — these investments are planned to reduce costs by either improving the efficiency of the business or altering its cost structure. This can be achieved by improving existing processes or by radically altering them. The processes affected could be in any areas of the business, e.g. production, administrative, distribution, etc.

The financial justification of these projections is easier to prove than for some of the other types of investment decision. This is because existing costs are known and new costs can be relatively easily calculated. The risks attached are generally small and identifiable as many of the aspects related to the decision are under management's direct control.

*Revenue earning investments can be categorised as*:

(A) **Expansionary** — investments to support business expansion can take an infinite variety of forms, primarily aimed at taking advantage of growing demand in an existing market, or improving the organisation's market share in its own markets or, in order to penetrate new markets. The critical assumptions on which decisions *vis-à-vis* expansion will be based are those related to the markets concerned. Assimilating relevant, accurate and timely knowledge about markets will be very important here. As markets are highly volatile and the activities in the market-place are largely outside management's control, the level of risk attached to assumptions about the market is very high. Projects will no doubt be the subject of ruthless scrutiny and detailed risk analysis will be carried out. The criteria for appraising this type of investment are many, including both quantitative and highly qualitative aspects.

(B) **Restructuring** — this form of investment is often seen as being carried out for defensive purposes. It is normally carried out to either consolidate a position in the market-place, to alter or change cost structures or to enhance efficiency. Examples might include changing geographical location, selling off non-trading related assets, e.g. property, building new factories, investing in different distribution networks and altering methods of communication, to mention but a few. Investment criteria will be similar to that of cost saving and expansion depending upon the amount of the proposed spend, the potential consequences and the types of assumptions on which the proposal is based. Restructuring decisions that go awry can be fatal to the organisation.

(C) **Replacement** — the replacement of assets can be either revenue or non-revenue earning. Whatever the consequence, replacement activity is fundamental to the continued profitability of the business. A major difficulty faced by organisations is the level and timing of the replacement speed. This will be reviewed in the context of the business activity concerned and the potential impact on levels of profitability.

## 9.4   AN INVESTMENT DECISION CONCERNING EXPERT SYSTEMS

We have already discussed the high risk element attached to expert systems development. What we need to now consider is how one could possibly classify an expert system project, how we could identify and measure the returns and the criteria needed in order to motivate the project.

### 9.4.1   Classification of an expert system project
An expert system is likely to be one of

— a cost saving
— expansionary

— replacement, or
— 'something in between'

investment. A 'something in between' project is one where the benefits do not clearly stand out or they (the benefits) are too subtle to monitor and thus to measure. In the long run they are likely to demonstrate their advantages in many different ways. An example would be any form of investment aimed at enhancing motivation, or improving employee loyalty.

The benefits take a while to manifest themselves and when they do they are difficult to measure. One might be able to relate a reduction in employee absenteeism or an increase in productivity thereto and thus find ways of establishing the extent of the returns in a quantitative fashion.

These types of projects can have an enormous indirect spin-off by improving communications and by enhancing corporate culture.

Examples of the types of Expert System projects that might form part of the organisation's overall investment profile are described in Table 9.1.

Table 9.1 provides some ideas on potential expert systems applications that may contribute to cost saving investments of the organisation. What needs to be borne in mind is that expert systems have a far greater contribution to make than decision support systems (refer to Chapter 6). The expert system *proposes* a solution by selecting an *optimal* alternative based on the rules included in its knowledge base. Therefore, whenever an expert's selection procedure is required (subject to the other constraints set out in Chapter 8), an expert system can provide some very powerful input into the decision-making process. Allied to this, a meaningful expert system application is not difficult to find and can fit in quite comfortably with other organisational investment projects.

*Cost saving by altering the cost structure* is achieved by

— altering the fixed cost base of the organisation
— changing the variable cost element of the products or services offered
— amending the distribution of costs by altering their collection points, e.g. increasing expenditure on marketing and reducing it on inventory holding costs
— eliminating certain costs altogether, e.g. selling goods and services at a different point in the distribution channel thus taking a smaller monetary profit, however eliminating certain costs.

Technology, and especially information technology, plays an enormous part in the altering of the cost structure of organisations. This is very clearly evidenced in the financial services sector. Technology plays a vital part in the marketing, origination, pricing, delivery and execution of financial deals. The additional input by expert systems might be that of providing the personal expert adviser on the doorstep of every existing or potential client; this will certainly diminish the costs of a large marketing team, door-to-door salesmen and professional consultants.

| Aspect of the business | Potential expert system application |
|---|---|
| Inventory control | • Proposing alternative sources of supply<br>• Front-end to a DSS on optimal stock levels<br>• Proposing alternative customer service levels |
| Credit control | • Credit analysis of the customer organisation<br>• System highlighting currency exposures on foreign revenue accounts |
| Research and development | • Evaluation of R&D proposals<br>• Evaluation of suitable research techniques |
| Production | • Proposing alternative production systems<br>• Evaluation of product life cycles<br>• Identification of quality control problems |
| Marketing | • Evaluation of target markets and their possible consumer behaviour<br>• Evaluation of alternative forms of promotion |
| Distribution | • Vehicle scheduling system<br>• Proposal for optimal stockholding by location |
| Service | • Review of alternative service benefits to customers<br>• Diagnosis of equipment faults |
| Technology | • System selection procedure application<br>• Technology fault diagnosis |
| Administrative | • Schedule of order processing application<br>• System proposing alternative office procedures |
| Finance | • Risk evaluation system related to different projects<br>• Investment proposal system |

Table 9.1   Cost saving for increased efficiency.

To take our financial services example a step further, imagine the marketing power of an organisation that not only provides home banking services but a wide range of on-line expert investment advice? This could be an expert system that questions the user with regard to his personal financial profile. Based on this and the mix of investment services that the organisation has to offer, the system could recommend personal investment strategies to the inquirer and explain the reasons underlying its advice.

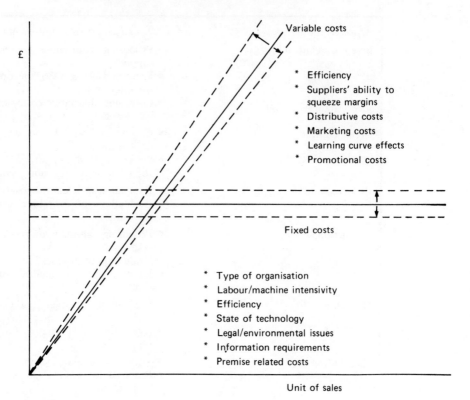

Fig. 9.2   Typical business cost structures.

Figure 9.2 sets out some of the factors that influence the cost structure of organisations. Of these factors some are within the ambit of management control and some are not.

**Expansionary** projects are those with the most strategic effect on the organisation. Here expert systems can play an important role too.

Expert systems designed to play a role in strategic planning are likely to be complex. This is because several experts from different functions need to be involved so that the expertise across the disciplines of the organisation can be harnessed. The power of an integrated expert planning tool could however, be immense.

Replacement projects could also include the use of expert systems. Here their contribution could be one of evaluating different replacement alternatives; diagnosing, debugging and/or monitoring system behaviours or planning equipment replacement across the organisation.

The 'something in between' projects, defined here as being those where the payoffs are not altogether clear, are potentially infinite in number. As was suggested under the heading 'The first application', organisations are well advised to begin their exploration into expert systems by selecting an application where the returns are modest, small or are not directly

| Form of expansion | Potential expert system application |
|---|---|
| Increased capacity (people/machines) | • Diagnostic of resource requirements under different capacity alternatives<br>• Planning the development of increased capacity |
| Geographical spread | • Evaluation of different locations based on given criteria<br>• Diagnosing resource requirements |
| New products | • Predictor of new product profiles to match researched consumer behaviour<br>• Design of new product packaging |
| New markets | • Evaluation of new markets, for example costs of entry<br>• Training sales staff on selling techniques |
| Increased market penetration | • Monitoring of market share gains or losses<br>• Interpreting consumer behaviour and consumer preferences |
| Merger/acquisition | • Evaluating target companies<br>• Planning different courses of action under different scenarios |

Fig. 9.3

measurable. Examples could include:

• staff procedures manual
• clarification of any type of legislation relevant to the business or to the employees of the business
• a range of systems/or education and training tools
• details of quality control standards
• monitoring of actuals against planned results and expert recommendation given on how to address any significant variances.

### 9.4.2   Establishing criteria for the expert system investment decision

An expert system project is likely to be financed out of the funds that the organisation has earmarked for long-term capital investments. The criteria for deciding whether the investment should be made need be no different to any other software development project. The financial analysis and risk analysis can be carried out by employing conventional methods. Conventional methods include detailed analysis of:

• the incremental net cash benefits that may be potentially earned as a result of the investment decision
• those factors that are most sensitive to the macro- and micro-environment when predicting the likely future outcome of the project — commonly referred to as a sensitivity analysis

- the timing of the cash inflows and outflows and the risks related thereto
- the overall risk profile of the project as regards both the earning of revenue and the incurring of costs
- the relevant qualitative aspects that are peculiar to each investment decision
- the opportunity cost or cost of capital related to the project

As has already been pointed out, the capital investment decision is among the most difficult decisions facing management. An investment in an expert system is akin to most investment decisions except that the benefits and the costs are currently extremely difficult to quantify in advance.

The cost that is likely to be a substantial element of the investment and one that is difficult to quantify will be of the soft costs associated with the experts' time as well as any other related opportunity costs. The only advice that can be given here is that the organisation should plan very conservatively.

**Monitoring** the expert development system will be discussed in Part III under stages of expert system development.

### 9.5   AN EXPERT SYSTEM TO ASSIST IN THE EVALUATION OF CAPITAL EXPENDITURE

**Motivation**
An expert system of this nature might be useful to organisations that are capital intensive and make frequent and significant decisions with regard to the capital expenditure that their type of business demands. An example might be a construction business that has numerous construction sites in different geographical locations. Part of the business might be the investment in various items of plant and equipment and other capital items.

*Objectives of the system*
To provide expert advice on the capital investment decision. The system should assist in the approval and selection of projects as well as explaining the criteria applied in order to grant funding approval.

*Anticipated benefits*
The benefits to be gained by developing the system are as follows:

(a) The financial director and the financial controller will be able to delegate some of the initial appraisal stages to a junior who will be advised and guided by the system. This will save them a fair amount of time due to the volume and frequency of capital investment applications.
(b) The expertise required in order to evaluate the proposals put forward will be formalised and available for review and questioning.

(c)  An *aide-mémoire* is provided (by the system) to those carrying out the investment evaluation. This will assist them in taking due consideration of pertinent aspects of the investment decision and the consequent recommendation *vis-à-vis* the allocation of funds.

(d)  A logbook or record is kept of all applications, their details, a record of the responses to the system generated questions and the decision recommended.

(e)  The organisation will gain as a result of formalised, standard procedures accessible to all concerned.

(f)  The system could be linked to a spreadsheet program that is designed to carry out the quantitative analysis and any sensitivity analysis that the expert system might recommend.

(g)  Relevant investment criteria appropriate to the investment decision will be taken cognisance of, and a record kept of what these criteria might be with regard to each application.

### Relevant organisation critical success factor (CSF)

The organisation's critical success factors have been identified among other things as

- astute contract tendering
- efficient control of costs
- meeting contract deadlines

The development and implementation of an expert system that assists in the capital expenditure decision will directly help the organisation in achieving these CSFs. As a substantial part of the costs incurred are related to capital expenditure items, formalising the appraisal methodology and making the system accessible to the relevant staff will speed up the filtering process.

### Time taken

The time normally taken in order to review a capital expenditure request can take anything between one and ten hours. The majority of cases typically take an average of one to three hours. The number of requests processed monthly ranges between fifteen and twenty applications. This means that the time taken up in evaluating capital expenditure decisions without the benefit of an expert system is at least 30 hours a month.

### Task responsibility

This is usually handled by the financial director aided by the financial controller. The preparation of the capital expenditure request is the responsibility of the operational managers assisted by their accounting staff.

The quality of the information provided in support of a capital expenditure request is most often extremely poor. An inordinate amount of time is spent by the financial controller in obtaining adequate information to decide whether to allocate the necessary funds.

### Knowledge input to the expert system (ES)

The knowledge to be encapsulated in the ES will include *inter alia*:

- Knowledge about the organisation, its businesses, the operating divisions and the type of contracts that they are involved in.
- Knowledge about the appropriate criteria required for different types of investment.
- Knowledge about the types of returns that can be expected and the likely risks attached thereto.
- Knowledge about the timing of the investment as well as the terminal or exit realisations if these are possible.
- Knowledge about the setting of priorities with regard to investment decisions.
- Knowledge about the best methods of financing different types of investments.
- Knowledge of the taxation benefits available to different types of investments.
- Knowledge of the key qualitative issues that need to be heeded in the investment appraisal.

### Project classification

A cost-saving project aimed at improving organisational efficiency.

### Expert

The expert who has volunteered to develop the system is the financial controller. He will work under the supervision of the financial director. Other members of the board, e.g. the director of projects and the marketing director will act as consultant experts throughout the system development.

### The knowledge engineer

This will be Joe Smith who is seconded from the IT department for the duration of the project. He has a certain amount of experience with expert systems and has the programming knowledge to integrate the system with the rest of the organisation's systems.

### The users

It is envisaged that the main users will be operational managers who will use the system to see whether their applications for capital equipment will meet the basic criteria set by the system. The system will advise them on whether their applications will be put forward for recommendation to the financial director, or if the investment is large enough, to the board.

The users will have direct access to the system (by Password control) and will thus get their initial screening without having to await on the availability of the financial controller or financial director.

### Software

The software tool to be used is ◄◄◄◄◄◄
The cost of this tool is ◄◄◄◄.

*Estimated time to develop the prototype*

This is estimated to be 24 man-weeks, which includes 10 weeks of the expert and 14 weeks of the knowledge engineer. The estimated salary cost is ◄◄◄◄◄.

*Summary of costs*

Time        ◄◄◄◄◄
Software   ◄◄◄◄
Hardware   ◄◄◄◄
Other      ◄◄◄◄

Total (say)   45 000

*Estimated quantification of benefits*

This can be taken as 30 hours a month multiplied by twelve months = 360 hours.

Assuming the cost per hour of the staff tied up is on average 25 then the benefits per annum are at least £9000.

The payback period (ignoring qualitative aspects) is five years.

# 10

# Enlisting the appropriate experts

It is out of the personal experiences of acting as a domain expert for different Expert Systems that this chapter is written: it would appear that no currently available literature expresses similar first-hand practical experience in expert systems development.

## 10.1   IDENTIFYING THE APPROPRIATE EXPERTS

There are many very different experts existent within most organisations. They either reside in different parts of the organisation, e.g. production as opposed to administration; they are knowledgeable in many different areas and they display their expertise in a variety of ways. Some expertise is very evident and some far less so. The experts playing a large role in the mainstream of the business, e.g. marketing staff or consultants, are more visible than those that obstensibly *support* mainstream activities, e.g. the toolroom engineers or the laboratory technicians. Sometimes the more visible experts are of the more outspoken type but this is not necessarily so. Furthermore the more outspoken or more extrovert experts are not necessarily the *best experts*, nor the ones most able to *articulate their expertise*. In developing an effective, appropriate and meaningful Expert System it is necessary to harness the skills of an 'available, articulate and co-operative' expert. Experts (good ones) are those people with the least time to explain how they do their work. Furthermore, they are often unable to explicitly articulate their expertise in a form that can easily be structured into a system that will reproduce this knowledge.

It is a known saying in the world of expert systems — '*No expert, no expert system!*' The obvious implication is that the expert and what he has to contribute are the critical ingredients of the whole system.

The big question facing many managers is: how in fact does one identify the appropriate expert? What in fact is the definition of an expert in a practical context? Another important question is: who is the most suitable expert for a particular application? All of these questions are very important when enlisting the *right* expert to participate in a particular project. Here are some very broad guidelines which can be applied in rooting out the *right* expert who is prepared to *commit* both *time and effort* towards the development of live expert systems:

— enlist the expert who can articulate his knowledge in a reasonably structured and clear manner. This will give the knowledge engineer (see next chapter) an opportunity to gain some understanding of the domain area being replicated. Filling out the knowledge, improving on its structure and enhancing the sophistication can be achieved more easily at a later stage;

— approach those experts who have taken the opportunity to verbalise their knowledge in the form of lectures, conferences, training courses, articles and books. These experts are likely to have had to consider not only how they can *represent* their knowledge, but they are most likely to have had to *reflect* on some of their cognitive processes. This will prove to be a great help to the knowledge engineer charged with replicating (where appropriate) the expert's thought patterns;

— ensure, in so far as possible, that the expert is recognised as such by at least his peers and superiors who operate in or interact with the expert's domain;

— involve an expert familiar with computers and the broad concepts of software technology. It is an added advantage if the expert *believes* that his expertise can be both expanded and enhanced by more and better use of information technology;

— appoint a 'support panel' of experts in similar or overlapping areas who would act from time to time as constructive critics of the expertise and the system structure;

— clarify with the potential experts well in advance the nature of the expertise that the system will require. As the range and depth of expertise varies to such an enormous extent between experts it is important that all concerned, especially the experts, understand exactly the scope of their intellectual challenge;

— clarify with potential experts the success rate expected of the system (see below expert systems as opposed to conventional systems);

— endeavour to select those experts least likely to be threatened by an apparently 'deskilling' process of the new technology. This is a difficult task to say the least. First of all one needs to consider the implications of *deskilling* someone and secondly, one is faced with the difficult prospect of 'counselling' those possibly involved through any misgivings that they might have. With regard to deskilling this is a very sensitive and subjective issue and for insecure and/or dubious experts this may/will prove to be a very real personal threat.

In order to put some of these thoughts into perspective it is necessary to point out some important points with regard to the concept of expertise; the difference between Expert Systems and conventional systems, and what can be reasonably expected of an Expert System. Let us look at these issues individually.

## 10.2   WHAT IS EXPERTISE?

This is considered to be the ability (intellectual, physical or otherwise) to demonstrate special skill or knowledge with regard to a subject, function or activity. These skills are above average in both their execution and the consequent results. Non-physical skill is most often associated with the ability to apply knowledge.

What knowledge is and what it embraces has been covered in some depth. What most often distinguishes an expert is his problem-solving techniques, evidenced by the ability to grasp very quickly and efficiency the essence of a problem, to see realtionships and to arrive at good solutions. Good solutions are those which provide better than average solutions in the majority of cases. The expert applies his knowledge by a very efficient process which utilises timing, sequence and use of combinations. It is this ability, i.e. a heuristic skill, which enables the expert to solve problems effectively which would otherwise suffer from combinatorial explosion. The expert's main ability lies in very quickly translating and sorting information and then applying a personally developed rule base to identify relevant relationships that offer an optimal solution.

What one must bear in mind is that the expert is not always right; what he proposes is not always totally right; he is learning all the time and his knowledge and the way he applies it changes with time and experience.

---

**An expert**

- identifies issues relevant to the problem
- solves complex problems
- explains the results and how these were arrived at
- learns continuously and restructures knowledge
- identifies exceptions (which can be as many as there are rules)
- applies not the absolute letter of the rule but rather its spirit
- IS HUMAN!

---

## 10.3   THE DIFFERENCE BETWEEN EXPERT SYSTEMS AND CONVENTIONAL SYSTEMS

Expert systems have much in common with conventional systems but they are not the same. The differences are important and need to be recognised in the design, building and implementation processes.

First and foremost the *objectives* of an expert system are not the same as those of conventional systems. A conventional system is built to perform some useful task and is expected to perform the task correctly or to arrive at the right answer every time.

A human expert is not expected to be right every single time, nor can the systems designed by the expert be any better. A good comparison here is with algorithmic decision support systems, which analyses data and/or information in a prespecified fashion. The answers supplied, if the system is working correctly, are entirely accurate. The inputs provided may, however, not have been appropriate to the decision. The information analysed may in fact have been the wrong type of information or it may have been analysed in the wrong way.

Let us take an example:

XYZ Fashion Retailers is keen to prepare for the following season's fashions. They have decided on the style of the garments and the colour combinations. They now need to plan for the mix of the range that they wish to hold; optimal stock-holding levels have to be set by both quantity and location; re-order levels need to be set and potential stock-holding costs require calculation.

Decision support systems can provide a lot of the input data to the decisions that need to be taken. They can for instance

— analyse what occurred in previous seasons;
— calculate correlations between different items which may indicate cause and effect;
— calculate optimal mixes based on criteria such as for instance cost, lead times and geographical location.

All of this can provide very helpful input into the decision-making process. So how do the experts respond? They take all the relevant information known to them and to that apply lessons learned from experience, intuition and special knowledge which they might have, e.g.

- how the competitors handle this process
- which stores have the most motivated sales staff who will increase store throughput
- stores in cities require a different range and mix to those in urban centres and to those in the country
- some ranges sell best via mail order
- the annual budget has just been announced which will increase the spending power of the man in the street
- in the previous year in general the public were purchasing clothes several sizes bigger than their normal body size,

and so on.

Based on this 'compiled knowledge' the expert will make some far-reaching decisions. The information provided for decision-making may have been totally correct and yet some bad decisions could follow.

Whether the above example lends itself to an expert system would entirely depend on the specific circumstances of the organisation. Bear in mind that the power of the expert system is that when it proposes a solution it can explain the criteria used and the conclusions reached on the way to arriving at that solution.

### 10.4   WHAT CAN BE REASONABLY EXPECTED OF AN EXPERT SYSTEM?

It is vital that the expert who will act as domain expert understands what is expected of the system that he is building. The objectives must be very clearly set. It is also important to establish at the outset how the performance of the system will be judged. This can clearly only result after several (many) interviews with the system rather than just one or a few. An expert builds credibility over time. Likewise so must the expert system —however, over *far less* time.

One of the prime functions of an expert system is to *transfer* knowledge. The emphasis thus lies in eliciting the procedural decision-making process of the expert and representing them in the system in such a way that they are clear and can be readily followed and understood. This challenge falls to the new breed of systems analyst/engineer whose role it is. The tasks of the knowledge engineer will be discussed at length in the next chapter.

### 10.5   ARTICULATING KNOWLEDGE

This is a fundamental issue to the development of expert systems. Firstly, as mentioned, some experts are more articulate than others. Secondly, even articulate, highly experienced experts can seldom spontaneously explain which part of his knowledge he applies to the solving of a problem. More difficult still is how his internal 'inference engine' operates.

Imagine if one were to confront a room full of randomly selected people with a time-constrained task, the task being to set out, in writing, the essence of their jobs or what they are most taken up with every day. They would then be requested to devise a rule base which should clarify how they tackled their activities. This rule base should be self-explanatory! This type of experiment might provide some interesting results.

In essence this is what the expert is being called upon to do. The expert is aided by having the scope of the area of interest very carefully defined. Articulation of his knowledge will also be prompted and 'mined' from his brain by a knowledge engineer. The knowledge that typically pours forth from the expert is likely to be ill-specified or incomplete. It will also be expressed in an unstructured fashion where links and relationships are not immediately clear. The more experienced the expert, usually the better the articulation of knowledge. The better the knowledge engineer at his task the *more* expertise can be extracted from the expert.

## 10.6   USING MULTIPLE EXPERTS

There is normally more than one expert with regard to a potential application area. While it is important to let them all feel in some way involved, they can in no way all be involved all of the time. It is advisable to start off with a single expert in order to collect the ground rules of the knowledge and to get some feel for its boundaries. It is best to try to identify the most *articulate* expert to act as the pioneer. Later on in the project other experts could be involved so as to 'enrich' the set of rules already obtained and to check out the correctness and consistency of the solutions proposed.

Involving multiple experts will be further developed in Part III under Preparing the Organisation for Expert Systems.

## 10.7   MOTIVATING THE EXPERTS

Usually people are fascinated with knowledge and know-how, not least by their own. Very often they do not have the ability, time, and/or inclination to reflect on the power of know-how in carrying out daily decisions or the running of the business. We often refer to someone as having 'nous', and infer that it is the people with nous who make things happen. If the concept of expert systems is approached correctly, the experts carefully educated in what the potential of the tool is and where the constraints lie, motivation will be evidenced in being both willing and anxious to participate.

As has been pointed out, expert systems are suitable for tasks that benefit from the results of experience and/or could potentially suffer from combinatorial explosion. Explaining this point to experts is important as it provides them with a better feel for the relevance of their 'knowledgeable' input.

Motivating experts to participate in a project will be largely affected by *inter alia*

— the manner in which the concept is introduced to them
— the level of senior management commitment clearly demonstrated
— their own self-confidence and the recognition awarded to them as an expert
— their general disposition towards information technology
— their willingness to learn, explore and seek new horizons.

Somewhat surprisingly know-how experts resident in the organisation exist in many often unexplored corners, and it is often these unrecognised experts who are happy to participate in experiments and new projects.

### 10.7.1   Will experts feel deskilled?

Deskilling is the term used when a process is mechanised, automated or otherwise transferred from a human. A person who believes he holds a special skill is likely to unreasonably defend against this process, a fact often pointed out by behavioural scientists, trade unions and experts themselves. No system will ever replace the judgement of a human being; though the more repetitive tasks will be taken from them, giving greater time and opportunity to perform more challenging and meaningful tasks. Experts and others should not only be more informed, but wiser as a result of the use of expert systems.

Figure 10.1 sets out the '*The Expert transition curve*'. This has been developed as a result of the author's experience as an expert, combined with feedback gained from other experts and knowledge engineers. The importance of the role of the knowledge engineer in motivating the expert can be illustrated here too.

**The expert's transition curve** is a guide to the changes in motivation over time. The knowledge engineer can play a large role in smoothing out the curve, i.e. diminishing the peaks and troughs and reducing the time element.

The shape of the curve, the stages through which the expert is likely to pass and the duration within the different stages is usually affected by

— the manner in which the expert was introduced to expert systems
— the support of management
— the confidence and abilities of the expert
— the skills of the knowledge engineer
— the understanding of the objectives set and the manner in which these are
   to be achieved

### Stage 1 — trepidation
Most experts, no matter how confident, have a certain amount of trepidation with regard to building an expert system. Part of the trepidation will naturally be with respect to how they see themselves and how this new challenge will influence the way others see them. Trepidation is usually experienced as a mixture of fear and excitement. It is considered to be a healthy emotion especially when tackling something relatively new and unknown. Most experts start from this point.

### Stage 2 — excitement
In this first stage motivation soars. The expert has an idea of the objectives set and the first few paces seem to take him in immeasurable leaps closer to achieving those objectives. He gets a feel for the technology and starts marvelling at his own thought processes. This feeling is heightened as the first rules are played back to him and the power of the tool starts emerging.

### Stage 3 — disillusionment
During this stage the initial excitement has worn off. The progress has slowed down immensely. The combinatorial explosion problem might have presented itself. The expert starts getting tired of articulating everything in rules. He starts having difficulty in explaining some of his more intuitive reasoning. The system's objectives become increasingly blurred. Structuring difficulties might occur.

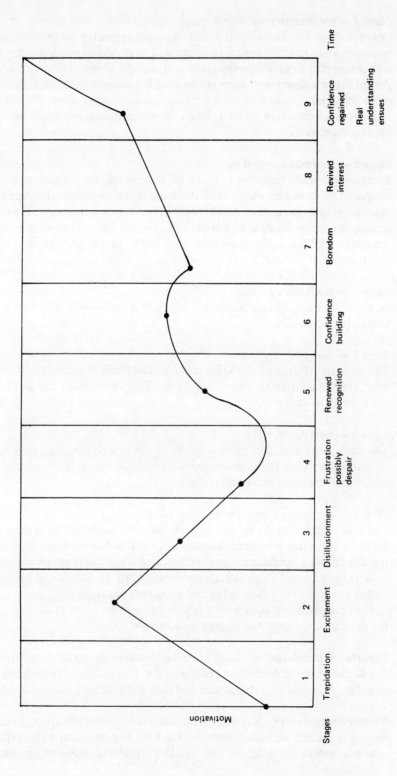

Fig. 10.1  The expert's transition curve.

### Stage 4 — frustration (and even despair)

Frustration sets in. The nadir is usually reached during this stage. Possibly the structure was wrong or requires alteration. The expert's knowledge can seem rather superficial and inconsequential at this stage. Often, it is just during this period that managers and users are looking for a demonstration. The expert often starts asking whether this was an appropriate application after all. The objectives become very blurred. Team work is critical at this point and many experts drop out.

### Stage 5 — renewed recognition

Something usually happens to reinstate the expert, the objectives and the system. This could be the skill of the knowledge engineer, the support of management or the enthusiasm of the users. Whatever the cause, the expert shakes off his antipathy and makes renewed efforts. There is renewed recognition of what the objectives should be, the opportunities and the constraints.

### Stage 6 — confidence building

As a consequence of Stage 5 confidence is built up again and there is a renewed sense of achievement.

### Stage 7 — boredom

The excitement is over as is the frustration. The grind of getting the system to work and the constraints of technology can inflict boredom. The fine tuning can seem pernickety.

### Stage 8 — revived interest

The back is broken. The system works albeit in a rough fashion. There is something to show. The system becomes a focal demonstration point and the real sophistication is about to proceed.

### Stage 9 — enthusiasm and real understanding

The expert feels that the marathon is all but over. He is master of this skilful tool which he has produced, nurtured, loved and sometimes hated. The reality of how he can relate to an expert system is a unique experience to him.

Next time he will know better, start differently and above all have more realistic expectations. Now where is the next application ... ?

The reason for highlighting the possible transition curve of the key expert involved in developing the system is as follows:

**Experts**   Potential experts need to realise that developing an expert system is not all plain sailing. It can be a gruelling task. It may help to realise that they might go through these stages and that they will emerge if their persevere.

**Knowledge engineers**   Knowledge engineers could do well to recognise what the expert might be going through. They do not only assist the expert in articulating his knowledge but they need to facilitate and counsel him through some of the gruelling stages. The empathy of the knowledge engineer can be vital to the performance of the expert.

**Users**   Users must be sufficiently in the know of how the expert system is being developed so as to have realistic expectations of both the system and the expert. User support can be akin to an intravenous dose of vitamins to the expert. Their support, advice and help will raise the whole level of the motivation curve.

**Management**   It is important that management understands some of the stresses being faced by the expert. So often management, ignorant of what might be happening within the expert, will apply pressure, act negatively or worse still down rate the importance of the task. Instead they should endeavour to enhance motivation by uniting expert(s), knowledge engineer, users and management in a united endeavour.

## 10.8   THE EXPERT'S VIEW

### 10.8.1   Deskilling
This will not occur. On the contrary people can and will learn more by reflecting on their own though processes. No system can judge when the results are unreasonable. Systems need to be kept alive, to be updated and amended. Expert human judgement will always be required.

### 10.8.2   Sharing knowledge
This is a rewarding experience for the expert. He will have gained increased confidence and new knowledge about himself and his existing knowledge. Although colleagues may disagree with some of his knowledge it is likely to be on the emphasis placed in issues, rather than the issues themselves. The fact that experts seldom agree 100 per cent with one another is well known. This usually does not deter an expert from holding certain views.

### 10.8.3   Interacting with the knowledge engineer
This needs to be a good experience. A healthy mutual respect is required as expert and knowledge engineer venture towards a mutual understanding. The method that the knowledge engineer uses for extracting the expert's knowledge requires to be empathic to the way the expert thinks. Third-degree tactics are inclined to put the expert off.

### 10.8.4   The users
It is very important that the expert understands what users expect from the system. The transfer of knowledge will simply not take place if the knowledge presented is not that which is required. Practical expertise is seldom written down and it is this added dimension to the knowledge base that makes expert systems so powerful.

Users should have an opportunity to see and comment on the system's progress at suitable stages. Their role is further explored in Chapter 12.

### 10.8.5   The expert and management

Management should reinforce the expert(s) efforts along the way. They should show an active interest in both progress and the stumbling-blocks. They should consistently demonstrate commitment to the project by giving it a high priority rating in terms of both resources and the expert's time. If management does not view the concept as potentially strategically powerful it will never be so.

### 10.8.6   Multiple experts

Some expert systems call for the input of more than one expert. This could be either because the subject area is so complex that it requires exploration and validation from a wide range of expertise, or because the importance of the correct solution being provided by the system is such that it needs to draw on the knowledge of more than one expert. A good example is that of expert systems for medical diagnosis. Developing such a system demands input from experts worldwide in order to provide sufficiently correct solutions. Another example might be in the area of mergers and acquisitions. This subject straddles the fields of, for example tax, company law, accounting, finance, business policy and even economics. No one person could be expected to be an expert in all of these areas.

Achieving co-operation from a number of experts is one challenge. Pooling their knowledge in order to build one cohesive system is another. It has been found that it is more difficult to sustain the motivation of a group of experts than just one who finds it easier to identify with the system.

From the knowledge engineer's point of view the best way to obtain expert's knowledge is to interact with them one at a time. The level of his interpersonal skills will determine how difficult or easy it will be to manage the experts.

The expert's view is a synthesis of the author's view reinforced by the *few* experts who have so far been involved in commercial expert systems developments.

# 11

# The role of the knowledge engineer

The contribution that can be made by a competent knowledge engineer to the creation of a meaningful expert system cannot be over-estimated. Many a suitable application will fail to meet user requirements as a result of poor knowledge representation. Although many software houses promote their expert system software as being an easy to use tool for beginners and experts alike, the refinement that can be added by an experienced knowledge engineer can substantially add to the end result. While the author has a certain amount of experience in building expert systems without specialised help the systems so developed have reflected this shortfall.

## 11.1   THE MEANING OF KNOWLEDGE ENGINEERING

Engineering is often defined as the application of known techniques to new problems. In the case of expert systems the known techniques are those of systems analysis and the designing and development of specific systems in order to meet specific needs. The new aspect with respect to expert systems is that of dealing with a new ingredient termed knowledge.

A knowledge engineer is faced with the task of acquiring the domain knowledge from the expert and with representing it in a meaningful manner within the system. The knowledge engineer is thus not only faced with the task of extracting the relevant knowledge from the expert, but is required to aid the expert in articulating his rule base which drives the handling of his knowledge, This is no mean task! In most cases the knowledge engineer is unfamiliar with the subject area of the expert — not to mention trying to understand the subtleties of expertise therein.

One often hears of the term, user-friendly. This much hackneyed phrase is taken to mean a system which users find easy to access, to manipulate and to handle. The task of the knowledge engineer is to make the expert system *very* user friendly. What this means is that not only must the system appear to be highly interactive but it should appear to be highly comprehensible to the user. In expert systems' parlance the user should experience knowledge transfer as a result of interacting with a particular system. Knowledge engineering can thus be defined as 'the process of acquiring (eliciting), representing and utilizing knowledge in a manner which readily imparts specific expertise, by means of a software system, from an expert to potential users of that system'.

## 11.2    THE SKILLS REQUIRED OF A KNOWLEDGE ENGINEER

The role of a knowledge engineer is still very much in the evolutionary stages. At present there exist preciously few experienced engineers that can speak with substantial experience. No formal training exists as yet that will prepare those for this new and fairly unstructured task. Currently many of those who hold themselves out to be knowledge engineers are self-ordained systems scientists or analysts who have some experience and wish to pursue this apparent calling further. Many knowledge engineers commence their new found careers by developing their own systems. While hands-on experience is always a good method for learning, this form of experience most often suffers from (a) finding an application that suits the engineer and not the users and, (b) lack of objectivity on behalf of the representation of knowledge. This could result in the knowledge engineer believing that knowledge extraction is easier than it is and, that once he has designed a system any other system will be as easy or as difficult. There is no question that the engineer will have learnt something from his own mistakes. However his greatest learning will be in the interacting with experts. This will be the best way for him to learn not only how they think but also how best their knowledge can be acquired from them. In a sense this is a bit of a vicious circle. The engineer can best acquire skills by developing many systems — and the progress of expert systems is impeded by an apparent shortage in skilled knowledge engineers!

So what then are the skills required of an effective knowledge engineer? Some people experienced in expert system developments say that the skills should include:

— proficiency with expert systems software (this should embrace both the software shells and operating environments available)
— a fairly high degree of computer literacy so that he might advise on the possibility of integrating systems
— psychological skills, i.e. the ability to enter into the expert's way of thinking (frame of reference) in an empathic manner
— open-mindedness and an ability to grasp new and different concepts quickly and effectively

— the ability to be directive without being over imposing. Communication skills are essential. The knowledge engineer needs to maintain a guiding hand over the project, to keep the momentum in a forward direction and to monitor the state of the expert's motivation. (Refer to the expert's transition curve in the previous chapter.)

In most cases the knowledge engineer's greatest contribution is to assist the expert in articulating his expertise in the most clear and easily understandable manner. Some argue that it is the knowledge engineer who actually articulates the knowledge. This view is being increasingly contested. It is countered that only the expert is in a position to verbalise his knowledge and that the knowledge engineer's role is to help the expert to explain his cognitive processes and his knowledge in a meaningful manner. The engineer thus requires a fairly wide range of skills, many of which are behavioural in nature.

If the knowledge engineer cannot establish a strong rapport with the chosen expert he is unlikely to develop a very effective system. Knowledge engineering is still very much in the developmental stages and the variety of techniques used by different practitioners are many.

## 11.3   THE KNOWLEDGE ENGINEER AT WORK

The job of the knowledge engineer is to support the expert in articulating and exercising his know-how (specific knowledge) in a manner which will be useful to potential users of that know-how. The knowledge engineer has to create a system that is intelligible to the expert and to the intended user. This is often a far more complicated task than it would first appear.

Structuring of the system is all important. Not only must it be fairly flexible and cover an acceptable range of alternatives but it should not be so wide that the knowledge captured appears to be facile.

First and foremost the knowledge engineer needs to have a very clear understanding of the objectives of the system, for whom it is intended and how the system is to be used. This can only be achieved by spending time with the users and management (if these are not one and the same) in order to understand their requirements and how they see the expert system actually working. As spelled out in the chapter describing the role of the users, it is very important that objectives and expectations are clarified at the commencement of the project. This does not mean that the objectives are cast in concrete and may not change. What is important is that all those involved start from the same base and that the knowledge engineer knows what is expected of him.

The next key task of the knowledge engineer is to participate in the identification of the expert who is to play the leading or initial role. This is important in that not only does the knowledge engineer have to interact very closely with this individual, but it will give him a feel for what constitutes expertise in the chosen domain area. While this process is going on the knowledge engineer needs to be investigating the subject area for his own purposes. Although he can in no way be expected to emulate the expertise of the expert he needs to have some grasp of the area so that he can work with him in a meaningful manner.

Most important is that the knowledge engineer is able to recognise when know-how is being expressed. It is the inherent know-how of the expert, how it is manifested and when it is used that the knowledge engineer needs to capture and encapsulate in the expert system. The strength and effectiveness of an expert system depends on the quality and quantity of the expertise (know-how) contained therein. The knowledge engineer is as much on trial as the expert!

Further aspects to the knowledge engineer's job include:

— acquiring the knowledge from the expert(s).
— structuring the system, i.e. designing the scope of the system and spelling out its limitation.
— representing the knowledge.
— controlling the system design so that the knowledge operates in a way similar to that of the expert(s). If the expert(s) cannot identify with the system then it has not achieved its task.
— planning the project stages and advising on suitable milestones at which point the project should be reviewed.
— providing input to budgeting and progress reporting.

The last point is an important one. The soft costs (e.g. the expert's time, opportunity costs) attached to expert system development are not only difficult to measure but are often omitted in the costing of the system. This can give developers a very wrong picture of the resources in fact required.

## 11.4   ACQUIRING THE KNOWLEDGE FROM THE EXPERTS

The development of an expert system is entirely dependent on the knowledge provided by the chosen expert. Many say that herein lies some of the greatest problems with expert system developments. They hold that experts are inarticulate, insufficiently forthcoming and have poor under-standing of their own thinking processes. Refer to 'articulating knowledge' set out in the previous chapter.

Some experts are distinctly better at expressing the constituent parts of their knowledge than others. The effectiveness and techniques applied by the knowledge engineer can radically improve (or hinder) the process of acquiring expertise in a usable form from the expert. There are several formal methods of knowledge acquisition. While these are listed below they shall not be expanded upon in any length. This will be left to the more technical books that will delve into the advantages and disadvantages of applying different methods.

Some well known techniques are:

(1) *Introspection*. This is where the expert acts as expert and knowledge engineer. By examining his own thought processes the expert builds a system which he believes effectively replicates his thinking processes. Many excellent systems have been built in this way. As a general rule systems do benefit from the involvement of an experienced knowledge engineer.
(2) *Interviewing*. This is the most often used technique. Here the knowledge engineer interviews the expert for a couple of hours taking notes. The knowledge engineer then takes the knowledge provided and builds the system in a manner which he believes is akin to the way the expert thinks. The expert is then given the opportunity to verify whether the system is an accurate reflection of his knowledge.
(3) *Observation*. Here the expert is placed under close observation while at work. The process most often involves the use of video tape-recording in order to analyse what the expert is doing and why.
(4) *Induction*. This is the process of converting a set of examples into rules. Software programs exist which can handle this procedure. The problem that sometimes exists with regard to this procedure is that the rules can be too facile to have any meaning.
(5) *Prototyping*. This is an extension of the interviewing technique. Here the expert works with the knowledge engineer in building a system. Both parties contribute to the system design; the expert uses the system to test the knowledge to be included therein, and the knowledge engineer aims at getting the structure right by modifying the system while interacting with the expert.

The prototyping method is becoming increasingly common. It has the advantages of maximising the interplay between the expert and the knowledge engineer, of amending the system *en route* and achieving some visible results very quickly. Prototyping also facilitates the monitoring of the project and the ability to revise the system objectives at certain suitable stages.

## 11.5   CHECKING THE SYSTEM

It is important to remember that the expert system will not perform better than the expert. The advice that it provides will be more consistent, but not of better quality, i.e. it can provide the best of the expert's advice all the time. The expert's advice may, however, not be the best available. The system is to be implemented to provide some form of expert advice to users and not purely to privide for the intellectual satisfaction of the expert or the knowledge engineer, thus the system must stand up to rigorous checking for them and by them.

Checking of the expert system thus needs to be carried out by:

— the expert
— the knowledge engineer
— the interested managers who have plausible vested interests
— the 'panel or consultant' experts
— specialists in related disciplines whose work possibly overlaps with that in
  the domain area
— a recognised representation of the users.

Each party is likely to check the performance of the system in line with their expectations, their objectives and their particular biases. In this situation the expert system is no different from any other software tool. Expectations almost always seem to be too high! Careful user and management involvement should, however, minimise this understandable failing.


## 11.6   IS THE EXPERT THE RIGHT EXPERT?

The appropriateness of a particular expert to a project will become fairly apparent throughout the stages of the project. Although the knowledge engineer is unlikely to have more expertise than the chosen expert he will very soon notice inconsistencies, lack of confidence, lost motivation or the evidence of a pseudo-expert. The knowledge engineer needs to be very close to the expert throughout the development phase and should be alert to the possibility that an expert may not be able to deliver in line with established objectives. The sooner the knowledge engineer calls a halt to a project that is losing control, direction or quality input from any members of the interested parties the better. The knowledge engineer is akin to the master of ceremonies — the smoother the show the higher the praise accorded to the artists, the more disorganised the show the greater the blame placed on the master of ceremonies.
   Another blunt rule:

---

If project is complex
   and expert is dubious
   and user is unsupportive
   then knowledge engineer is advised to reconsider the viability

---


## 11.7   IN SUMMARY

A polished, well presented expert system that is suitable for immediate implementation by users is most likely to have had the input of a skilled knowledge engineer. While experts can most certainly develop their own systems, there exists a distinct role for a knowledge engineer, who may only be consulted from time to time, as opposed to being involved in hands-on development throughout.

# 12

# The role of the users

An expert system is for the users, not the glorification of the expert. The success of the expert system is gauged by its usefulness to users. Satisfying user requirements is a difficult task. First, users often find it hard to specify their exact requirements because they are more aware of what they don't want than of what they do. This may well be the result of having had to adapt themselves to systems imposed on them in the past. Secondly, users are immersed in current problems, which makes it harder for them to take a more distanced and objective view. Thirdly, users' perception of what they require is clouded by their personal biases.

Management needs to consider how these issues will affect the quality of user participation.

## 12.1   USER INVOLVEMENT

The role of the users is fundamental to any expert system development. The greater their involvement and the more their needs are taken into account in the design of the system, the greater the chance of the system meeting its objectives. The role of the user is manifold. As Fig. 12.1 points out the user should be continuously involved in all stages of the expert system development. It is the user who will provide the most *essential* feedback as to the meaningfulness of the system; its usefulness; its role in organisational life, and the extent to which the knowledge supplied contributes to usable practical commercial sense.

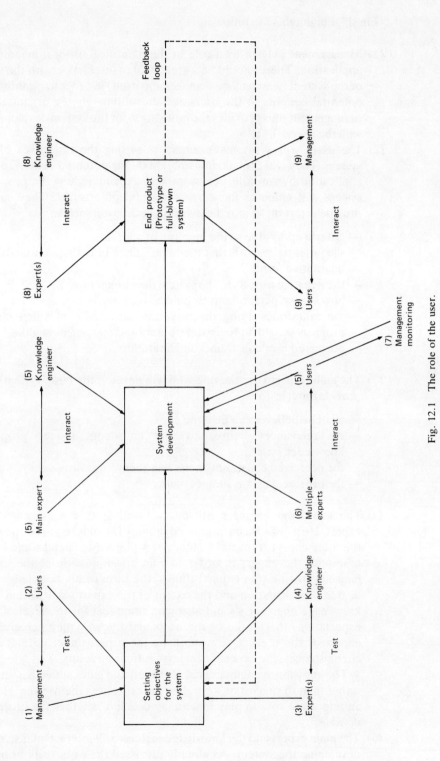

Fig. 12.1   The role of the user.

Fig. 12.1 highlights the following:

(1) **Management** plays a lead role in the identification of a meaningful application. There should be a great deal of interaction with the users of the system (who may be management itself) in order to establish the potential benefits to the users and thus ultimately the organisation. Management thus provides the motivation for the system development with the users.

(2) **The users** will assist, management in setting the objectives of the system. They will provide information on the potential benefits of the application by carefully reviewing and explaining how the proposed system will enhance the current method of practice. They should provide direct input into the investment decision such as

— criteria applicable to the investment appraisal
— the potential payoffs that might be gained in both quantitative and qualitative terms
— the negative aspects to the system development
— how system performance should be measured
— the milestones along the way, i.e. the stages at which system progress should be reviewed by users and management alike
— perceived user constraints and limitations

(3) **The main expert** (i.e. the one who will develop the basic system) will provide input as to

— what he believes can be done
— the relevance of his particular knowledge to the proposed knowledge base
— the perceived constraints as he sees them
— the project stages as he sees them

(4) The **knowledge engineer** will interact with both the users and the expert. He will gain a basic understanding of what is required and what the users expect from the system. He will need to spend some initial time with the expert in order to gain an impression of the expert himself, how he (the expert) thinks, the form of his knowledge, the degree of articulation and the extent of the expert's motivation. The knowledge engineer should also gain some feel for the level of user expectation, the profile of the users and the way they perceive the expert. If the users have no faith in the expert under normal daily circumstances, the expert system will suffer as a result.

The knowledge engineer is likely to test and guide objective setting, rather than to suggest or formulate the objectives themselves. He has an important role to play in actually deciding whether the project is *do-able*.

(5) The **main expert** and the **knowledge engineer** will interact intensively in developing the system. As already discussed the expert will bring his

know-how to bear and the knowledge engineer will structure this in the most appropriate manner to the type of system envisaged.

From time to time, either as a result of a pre-planned project timetable, and/or because practical sense dictates the need, the users should be consulted. They should be apprised of where it is at for the expert, e.g. where his problems or frustrations might lie; they should review the system development to date; they should review the objectives and test progress against their (the users) stated requirements. The users have a clear responsibility for guiding the development of the project. The rest of the team (expert(s), knowledge engineer and management) have a responsibility for giving them the opportunity of carrying this out both thoroughly and consistently.

(6) The **multiple experts** should also guide system development; they should test the validity and appropriateness of the knowledge provided by the main expert, and they should maintain open communication with the users. Meaningful participation on their part will enhance credibility of the overall system.

(7) **Management monitoring** of the system's progress is important from both a psychological and practical viewpoint. Management needs to be aware of team morale, the level of expert motivation and the state of user expectation. If these are negative or in a poor state the system is heading for disaster. Management concern, time and involvement can as always work wonders!

It is also necessary for management to understand the appropriateness of the objectives set and whether these require fine tuning, amending or major changes made to them. If so — it is during the system development stage that this should be recognised and not once the system is complete!

(8) **The expert(s) and the knowledge engineer** are responsible for delivering an end-product. The end-product may be a prototype system or a full blown system ready for user implementation. The system *never* ends there. It will always need improvement, updating and amendment so that the knowledge will not become redundant and that user requirements, which are continuously evolving, are met to the greatest extent possible.

(9) **Users and management** are the ones who will judge the efficacy of the system. If the users are satisfied the likelihood of management being satisfied is far greater. (The users and management may be one and the same depending on the type of application.)

Management is likely to review the whole process and not only attempt to measure the payoffs but to gain a general impression of the effect on the culture and performance of the organisation as well.

(10) **The feedback loop**. The feedback loop is introduced here in order to show that the learning process experienced by all those involved should serve to feed into and improve further objective setting and system development. This should necessarily hold for both new systems and the extended development of existing systems under review.

The very important point to consider with regard to expert system development is that there are many *different* users.

The expert(s), the knowledge engineer and the end user(s) are all users of the system in different ways. In many instances management is a user too. The users' perception of knowledge-based systems will directly affect the further identification of applications and the spirit within which these systems are absorbed into the strategic armoury of the organisation.


## 12.2   USER REQUIREMENTS

All systems are designed to meet perceived user requirements. The problem lies with the perception. Accurate and realistic perception is *only* achieved by spending *quality* time with the users in order to understand their needs better. This holds equally for any form of information system, expert systems being a *knowledge*-based rather than an information-based system.

It goes without saying that if there are no users of a system, why have the system? If the system does not meet user requirements there will be no users!

It would seem that a large portion of current commercial software applications are product rather than market led. This implies that the technology and the development of the product as decreed by technologists, and product originators is driving the product development rather than the market and the potential users. This rather non-market oriented bias is typical of many technological developments. Expert system applications are especially 'guilty' of this type of development.

The users of an expert system are likely to *have* very specific requirements of the system. Due to the high degree of interaction between man and machine it is essential that the system is *user friendly* (see Chapter 11 on Knowledge Engineering).

Users of expert systems can seek to satisfy one of several needs. For example:
— the user is acting in the place of an expert and is guided by the system
— the user is a trainee and is hoping to gain know-how and expertise quickly
— the user wishes to understand the extent of the knowledge inherent in an organisation
— the user wishes to be guided in the organisation's methodology of performing a function or carrying out a task
— the user might want to understand where faults could occur, say in equipment, and how the expert system copes with these faults
— the user might be an expert himself. He might use the system in order to learn from other experts, or he may wish to add to the knowledge base so as to broaden out or deepen the domain area
— the user might use the system as an *aide-mémoire* when carrying out an activity in the same domain areas as that of the system.

As commercial expert system applications evolve their potential use to the system users will also evolve. New types of applications will become acceptable as users understand better how to exploit the software technology.

Hitherto most users of information technology have been those who are involved with its data-processing capability. Here the information systems are largely used as a means to an end and not as an end in itself. The evolution of DSS and now expert systems is changing the way users view and employ information technology. As users become more comfortable with the idea of DSS and ES which assists them in the actual thinking part of the decision-making process they will become increasingly sophisticated buyers and users. In most other forms of industry, e.g. retailing, insurance, finance and consultancy, the sophistication of users is changing the accepted practices. The users/consumers are driving the forces of competition, the product offerings and the pricing structure of an industry. Expert system developers need to take heed that the *user* is *king*.

## 12.3   GETTING USERS TO DEFINE THEIR REQUIREMENTS

Users need to be actively encouraged to define their specific requirements of the planned expert system. This should include:

— what they would like the system to do
— how access to this compiled knowledge base will assist them in their performance
— the scope of the system as they see it
— the manner in which the system will be used
— the constraints and limitations of the system
— proposals with respect to implementation, the timing and the different phases thereof.

## 12.4   USER ACCEPTANCE

Getting users (end) to accept expert systems into the organisation is an aspect that will be expanded upon in Part III — Preparing the Organisation for Expert Systems.

Being involved in expert systems' development should be seen by the users as a positive development that will help them in job performance. Users should not be allowed to consider this new technological development as a threat to their jobs. As far as the author is aware, and she has discussed this with many people in the field, no one has been replaced by an expert system in carrying out a job. The system is a tool, aimed at *supporting* the user in his task and *not* acting as a human *substitute*.

Management needs to make this quite clear to users from the start. Users need to be reassured that their contribution, skills and knowledge are valued. Users should be introduced to the expert system concept carefully and in a well thoughout manner. Resistance to change is a human trait.

## 12.5   EXPERT SYSTEM IMPLEMENTATION

The success of the implementation programme will depend *entirely* on the extent of user interest and user involvement from the commencement of the project. Commencement is considered to be in the early conceptual stages and *not after* the objectives have been set.

If the users have been involved from start to finish of the project they will normally advise on and devise their own implementation plan as they see the product evolve. A user defined implementation plan always has the greatest chances of support and therefore success.

No hard and fast guidelines can be provided for efficient and successful implementation as each expert system project is different in terms of impact and scope. Suffice it to say that with any system — comprehension minimises apprehension.

# 13

# Recognising the limitations

Problems and limitations exist in the building of expert systems, some are unique to this new type of software tool and some common to almost all software developments. We are interested here in those particular to expert systems and how the problems can be overcome, or in some way diminished. It is important that those who wish to proceed with expert systems development reflect on the limitations in advance. This will help in not only recognising these in good time, but will also remind management and all those potentially involved to proceed with caution.

Let us first consider some of the difficulties in developing an expert system:

## 13.1  LACK OF RESOURCES

This might be in the form of competent personnel, appropriate software tools and/or organisational capital. Articulate, competent and confident experts who are eager to expose their knowledge while experimenting with a new form of software technology are not always as readily available as one might hope. Knowledge engineers are a new 'breed' of computer specialist. They need training and experience and this only comes with exposure to many different projects.

Other computer specialists versed in (Artificial Intelligence) AI or (Expert Systems) ES techniques may be required to integrate the ES system with other systems. The demand for AI and ES specialists is accelerating rapidly and at present there is a clear market shortage of these people.

Lack of organisational resources largely depends on the organisation's approach to the budgeting for an expert system development and the level of management's commitment.

## 13.2   EXPERT SYSTEMS TAKE A LONG TIME TO BUILD

The development of an expert system from conceptualisation to delivery takes a relatively long time. Chapter 15 explores the different stages of an ES development. Whether a prototype system or a full blown system, an effective system will take months rather than weeks to develop. The time required to build a system depends on the complexity of the problem and the number of people assigned to the application team. Careful project planning, full user involvement and motivated and committed experts will assist towards reducing development time.

## 13.3   THE HIGH EXPECTATIONS OF THE USER COMMUNITY

This problem has been addressed at some length. It must be recognised at the outset that expert systems are not the new panacea. They will be able to do some new things and they will also present some new problems. If user expectations are not realistic the end-product will never be perceived as being effective.

## 13.4   PLANNING AND DEVELOPING THE EXPERT SYSTEM
##          PROJECT

The problems that could arise here are:

(1) The problem that the expert system is designed to solve is too complex.
(2) The gap between an expert's knowledge and that of a non-expert is so narrow that the expert system does not contribute much to the problem application.
(3) The expert is not a suitable one for the system development, e.g. he is not a true expert, he is inarticulate, his reasoning is shallow.
(4) The domain expert has insufficient time to devote to the project.
(5) The domain expert has become so demotivated that his interest can no longer be refired.
(6) The domain expert and the knowledge engineer cannot establish a suitable rapport.
(7) The multiple experts get so carried away with arguing the basis of the knowledge that progress is hampered.
(8) The knowledge engineer is insufficiently trained for the job.
(9) The knowledge engineer has not taken enough time and care to understand user requirements.

(10) The knowledge engineer selects that tool with which he is most comfortable regardless of how appropriate it is for the system application.
(11) The users find the system difficult to use.
(12) The system becomes so unwieldy that it is difficult to modify or amend.

The above-mentioned problems are very real in the context of expert systems. Management's awareness and willingness to tackle these problems will greatly improve the chances of experiencing a successful system development.

## 13.5   CHOOSING A TOOL FOR BUILDING AN EXPERT SYSTEM

Identifying a meaningful application, defining the problem scope and selecting the appropriate tool for building the expert system are the most difficult decisions that need to be made. All the other aspects to the project could be suitably addressed, but if the software tool chosen is not appropriate for the task the end result is destined to be less than effective. Often a tool is chosen for the wrong reasons. For instance:

— it is the cheapest
— the tool is the most efficient and suitable one for the existing hardware
— the knowledge engineer is most familiar with a particular tool.

If you have decided you are going to go somewhere you next decide how you are going to get there. For example if you intend to go from Boston to LA you would hardly consider using a bicycle. On the other hand if you intended travelling from Oxford to Cambridge you would hardly contemplate taking a Jumbo! This might appear enormously trite and simplistic, however the use and abuse of software technology in general suffers from this apparent user/technology myopia.

Expert system tools are as yet still very much in the developmental stages. Tools have not been designed with specific problems in mind. Further, researchers are not even sure what types of features should be included in a tool so that it can handle certain problems.

There are essentially two types of tools currently available for constructing expert systems, namely expert system shells and high-level programming language environments.

A shell usually consists of an inference engine and an empty knowledge base plus some debugging and explanation facilities. The advantages of a shell are that they are fairly easy to use, relatively cheap and can speed up the development time. Users of expert system shells often complain that they lack power in controlling the logic of the system; that an inference engine successful for one type of application is not necessarily satisfactory for another; and that in some instances the knowledge representation is awkward.

High-level language programming environments do not provide the knowledge engineer with a single prefabricated inference engine. Instead they are presented with a large set of tools from which the knowledge engineer is to design and build a customised system suitable for the intended application. While this can lead to a more appropriate and sophisticated system it demands the skills of experienced programmers and takes a longer time for development.

The discussion on the choice and suitability of expert system technology is a long and technical one — inappropriate for our purposes here. Some guidelines on the selection of a tool are, however, proferred.

The following factors should be taken into consideration:

— the suitability of the tool with regard to the level of complexity of the knowledge to be handled and the task to be achieved
— the availability of tool support facilities
— whether the tool can handle any special requirements demanded by the application
— reliability
— maintenance aspects
— tool support facilities
— the ability to integrate the tool with the other hard- and software in the organisation.

### 13.6   MAINTENANCE OF THE EXPERT SYSTEM

It is important to bear in mind that the expert system needs to be maintained in much the same way as experts themselves need to keep abreast of their field. The system will lose its power once the knowledge it holds is outdated. This will result in loss of credibility, which will do just as much harm as if the expert no longer had relevant expertise.

At the outset, the expert, who is the driving force behind the development of the system should be aware that it requires continuous and meticulous maintenance.

### 13.7   EXPERT SYSTEMS AND CONVENTIONAL SYSTEMS

Most organisations have a relatively high investment in some part of the spectrum of information technology. They are also probably continuously re-evaluating what they have and how this can be improved upon. Decision makers are continuously in the middle of the decision-making process, amending and upgrading the technology and information technology mix.

Expert system developers, vendors of tools and AI technologists are inclined to describe expert systems' technology as requiring specialised hardware and software. Having a host of different software and hardware is quite naturally an anathema to the business manager.

Further, there is a need to integrate the new technology with conventional Data Processing. There would seem to be little achievement of this amongst current systems developers. In fact the integration of ES with conventional systems is a major challenge to software specialists. Only once this is proved to be achievable in an effective manner will expert systems gain an easier acceptance and more ready credibility.

The real power of ES to the organisation will only be fully experienced once the systems are integrated into the entire information systems armoury and offered to users on an on-line, distributed basis.

# Part III

## Getting Started
## (Putting Theory into Practice)

# 14

# Preparing the organisation for expert systems

Many might wonder why an organisation needs to be prepared for expert systems and what this actually means.

Firstly, it is not really the expert systems aspect which the organisation has to prepare itself for, but rather (as the Preface points out) the fact that we are moving towards a knowledge-based society. This new type of society in which there will be renewed recognition of people as knowledge workers, is going to place new and different strains on the organisation, the management and the workers. Exactly what these changes and the consequent strains are likely to be is not easy to predict.

There is a strong possibility that workers who have hitherto complained of apparent lack of managerial attention to their efforts, might find a sudden intense interest in those efforts. This possible over-correction could prove almost equally distressing.

The organisation does not need to prepare itself for expert systems *per se* but rather for the impact of the new focus on practical knowledge. As was pointed out in Part I — The Strategic Implications — expert systems are only *another* (software) tool which can be used by an organisation to its strategic advantage. What makes it such a unique tool with such a powerful and wide ranging impact is the fact that it is the latest form of information technology which can harness the strategic knowledge inherent in the organisation. Management needs to be aware of the implications of introducing expert systems into the organisation if this is to be handled properly and to maximum effect. To date most of the applications have been driven by technologists in the DP (Data Processing) department who have learnt about this new tool. In an endeavour to promote it they have developed applications that were suited to them and these have been highly technical ones.

What this book advocates is that business management should lead the technology and not be led by it. If management is going to control its own destiny, it needs to take a proactive approach towards managing the knowledge and information that it has available to it.

## 14.1   KNOWLEDGE-BASED SYSTEMS AND INFORMATION-BASED SYSTEMS

Countries, organisations and people depend upon knowledge and information in order to survive. Why? Because knowledge and information about ourselves and about others influences our behaviour. The organisation seeks to obtain as much knowledge and information about its environment as possible, as this will influence its behaviour towards its

suppliers
customers
competitors
employees
legislators
environmentalists
and so on

The organisation disseminates knowledge and information internally in order to influence the behaviour of shareholders, managers and employees. Systems (technological or otherwise) that are based on knowledge and/or information are thus designed to have a significant impact on behaviour. The extent to which this is achieved and whether it proves to be motivational or de-motivational will depend largely on the approach adopted by management, the extent of user involvement and the manner in which the systems are introduced. The introduction of any new system implies having to cope with the management of change.

## 14.2   THE MANAGEMENT OF CHANGE

Organisations are in a continuous state of change in order to adapt to their changing envinronment. The *specific* management of change comes about when an organisation has specified a change objective, i.e. it is going to alter or introduce a new aspect to its business. The wider the potential impact of the change the greater the need for a clear management of change programme. Generally, alterations and changes to any type of system, especially information systems, has a very wide impact. Effective introduction of knowledge-based systems will potentially affect very many people.

## 14.3   THE IMPACT OF CHANGE

Major organisation decisions are taken by the few, but many, many other people are affected. Those decisions that have enormous change impacts can cause an organisational climate charged with tension; and tension most often arouses resistance to change. That is the challenge to management — to manage that resistance. The most effective way is to create a climate in which resistance to change is constantly being converted into problem-solving opportunity-seeking energy. As managers well know, prolonged, unrelenting resistance to change can seriously undermine the health of an organisation.

The introduction of expert systems as a new strategic tool will face a certain amount of resistance to change just as most new systems do. Management needs to be aware of this and pre-empt this if possible. For the most part organisations are advised to move into knowledge-based systems slowly and carefully. This does not mean secretively and behind closed doors. It would also be shortsighted to give up the introduction of expert systems if the first application is not a success. How many organisations can boast the introduction of any system which does not have an element of teething problems, not to mention substantial initial implementation setbacks?

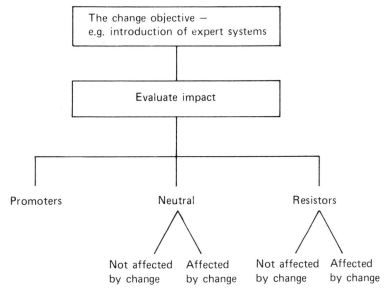

Fig. 14.1   The impact of change.

Change is usually driven by promoters who have different motivations for bringing about that change. The promoters of expert systems are likely to be management, experts, users and most often the technologists who currently have the best understanding of what they have to offer. The big caution that management needs to exercise here is that (a) expectations remain realistic and (b) the applications put forward are meaningful to all those involved.

The potential resistors to expert systems arise again for different core reasons — often not honestly voiced. These usually form two different contingents, i.e. those who will be directly affected and those who will be minimally affected or hardly impacted at all. The latter group are often the opinion leaders who feel that they have been insufficiently consulted and/or they resist any change on principle. The former group are likely to have some real issues that need addressing. However, both groups will have to be managed.

---

### THE RESISTORS

- **Some experts** (who fear undue exposure or deskilling)

- **Non-experts** (who fear further lack of recognition and even less opportunity to prove themselves)

- **The generally insecure** (Every organisation has a range of people who fall into this category)

- **Some technologists** (who may fear that if this technology is outside the DP department they will lose power and control)

- **Some users** (who resist computerisation in general and experience problems with the man–machine interface)

- **Training staff/management** (who may fear that self-tuition by interacting with the expert system will diminish their role)

- **The troublemakers** (Every organisation has a few of these. They ccould be the envious or purely those who wish to exert power)

---

Fig. 14.2.

The neutral parties are those who are either passive in nature, who are disinterested in how they carry out their task or who are unaffected by the change. Management needs to be aware whether passivity is in effect a total switch-off to the surroundings.

## 14.4  EVALUATING THE IMPACT OF INTRODUCING EXPERT SYSTEMS TO THE ORGANISATION

To get the most out of expert systems, management must take its introduction seriously. This means taking full account of the positive, negative and neutral effects on the organisation. Figure 14.3 sets out some of the possible areas that will be affected. The degree and extent of the impact will be influenced by the organisational climate. This will influence the reactions of those likely to be affected. Management needs to reflect on the key issues of likely concern and to identify and to interact with the people who will be affected.

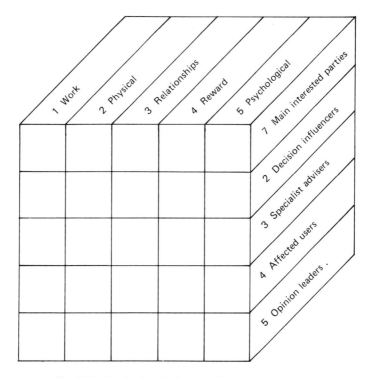

Fig. 14.3   Evaluating the impact of introducing expert systems.

## 14.5   KEY ISSUES RELATING TO EXPERT SYSTEM DEVELOPMENT (FIGURE 14.3)

(1) *Work*. Consider the likely changes in methods, procedures, quality, standards, timing and reporting as a consequence of expert systems.

(2) *Physical*. Consider the impact on people's physical environment. Will anyone be required to move office, transfer to other departments, work with different equipment, become more computer dependent?

(3) *Relationships*. Explore what could happen to existing work groups. Could there be promotions/demotions? Will peer group pressure alter? Could people be regarded differently? Will traditional hero roles change? This is important especially with regard to the experts.

(4) *Reward*. Consider what the pay-offs are to the organisation *and* to *all* the individuals potentially impacted. As well as the pay-offs, reflect on any trade-offs that may occur.

(5) *Psychological aspects*. Consider whether this new way of doing things might affect the value systems of the organisation and the individuals. This could be in the social need for belonging, ego and self-actualisation aspects on individuals. Particularly the expert(s) involved in system building are exposing themselves to new and wide criticisms that they could previously defend themselves against.

## 14.6   THE PEOPLE POTENTIALLY AFFECTED — THEIR CONCERNS, NEEDS AND DRIVES

(1) **Main interested parties** — these are likely to be:
  - management who make the decisions
  - those who have an interest in the outcome
  - those involved in using the system
  - those responsible for implementation
  - those responsible for maintaining the system

All of these parties need to be directly represented when management decides to make a decision affecting this area.

(2) **Decision influencers**. These are usually senior people who have a vested interest in not wanting or blocking a decision. They often wish to be consulted in great depth and are unwilling to carry the can for disappointing results.

(3) **Specialist advisers**. These are people who have knowledge and/or skills to help with the project. They often have vested interests too.

(4) **Affected users**. These are directly or indirectly affected by the introduction of expert systems. They are the ones who will operate the systems and will have a large say in the acceptance or rejection of the applications.

(5) **Opinion leaders**. These people exist at all levels within the organisation. They may not be involved in the decision but can have a huge influence over the smoothness of implementation. Ignore these people at your peril! They usually dominate the informal information system (i.e. the gossip network), they have persuasive powers and a very wide ambit of influence.

## 14.7   THE EXPERT SYSTEM'S TASK FORCE

It is a good idea to introduce expert systems to the organisation by getting together a group of people with a fairly clear brief. The group should represent people from all levels of the organisation. They should also emanate from a variety of functions preferably coming from different disciplines. All potentially interested parties (as set out above) should be involved generally with the 'task force' and specifically, once meaningful applications have been identified. The task force could be responsible for:

— investigating applications being developed by other organisations;
— investigating potential in-house applications;
— exploring the impact on the current technology used by the organisation;
— talking to users of potential systems;
— exploring areas of expertise with experts;

— identifying the CSFs of the businesses which are dependent on knowledgeable inputs.

The expert system task force should have a high rather than a low profile. They should also report to senior management who should be prepared to devote time to the findings that they will present.

The task force should be allocated a R & D budget so that the investigations can be detailed rather than superficial.

## 14.8   THE ISSUE OF SECURITY

The security of the knowledge entrapped in the expert system is going to be an important issue to the organisation. Soft and hardware technology specialists should be consulted on this aspect.

As always, management is advised to take the auditors along with them, so that the issue of security is adequately addressed.

## 14.9   LEGAL LIABILITY OF EXPERT SYSTEMS

This is a part of expert system development that has attracted a fair amount of comment and debate. Who is liable if the system provides the wrong or inaccurate advice? Is it the expert, the knowledge engineer, the system, the organisation? This debate cannot be discussed or settled here. It is important that management recognise that this issue could raise its head depending on the particular development.

---

**Possible reasons for resisting or accepting changes**

- Feared economic losses/anticipated economic gains
- Fears about personal security/hopes about personal security
- Fears about increased personal inconvenience/hopes of increased personal convenience
- Fears about decreased job satisfactions/hopes of increased job satisfactions
- Social fears/social anticipations
- Irritation with manner of handling the change/satisfaction with manner of handling the change

---

Extract from Arnold S. Judson, *A Managers' Guide to making Changes* (Wiley, 1966).

# 15

# Stages of expert system development and project management

The purpose of this chapter is to outline for management the most likely development phases of an expert system and how these can be most effectively monitored.

Parts I and II have spelled out what expert systems are and why they are important. The next step is really how to learn more about the actual building of a system and the operational details associated with implementing and integrating this new system. The current literature abounds with advice detailing different aspects related to systems development.

This chapter seeks to address the project management issues rather than expert system building techniques. As has been pointed out at length, the management of, and the support demonstrated by management, to the different stages of the system development will materially affect its overall success and acceptance.

## 15.1  PLANNING THE PROJECT

This phase is all important. The *proposed methodology* as set out in Chapter 8 outlines how management can:

(a)  identify a meaningful application
(b)  establish whether the appropriate experts are available
(c)  devise suitable objectives.

Detailed planning of the project further embraces assembling and costing all the likely ingredients; establishing a timetable with benchmarks for measuring progress; as well as setting out the firms of system testing; the system implementation stages and the types of maintenance it is most likely to require.

The *ingredients* of the project are likely to be:

(a) the project manager who will have responsibility for managing and monitoring the project as well as ensuring that both management and the users are apprised of progress at suitable intervals
(b) the expert
(c) possibly consultant experts responsible for validating the knowledge and the rule base developed by the primary expert
(d) the knowledge engineer
(e) the potential users of the system
(f) interested managers who have a vested interest in the development of the system
(g) the hardware and software which will be used to build the system

The people involved are often referred to as the application team. Some members will have more direct involvement than others, however all should feel some responsibility towards the smooth development of the system.

Costing the ingredients to be used is, as with most software developments, a difficult task. The hard costs (which include exact fixed amounts) do not usually present a problem. It is rather the soft costs that are most difficult to quantify and to value. Soft costs include, for example, the cost of peoples' time and the opportunity costs related to embarking on a certain activity. What makes the soft costs so difficult to plan for, is that invariably systems development takes longer than at first anticipated — no matter how conservative the budget is held to be. The reasons for this are manifold. In the case of expert systems it could be:

• that inappropriate objectives were set in the first place
• that the expert proves to be unsuitable
• that the knowledge engineer and the expert cannot reach sufficient accord in what they are trying to achieve
• that the consultant experts act more as a hindrance than as a help
• that user resistance proves a demotivating factor for the rest of the team
• that unsuitable software was selected with which to build the system
and so on.

These stumbling-blocks can prove to be very time consuming and thus costly.

Just as in any other financial exercise, the project manager should monitor actual progress and actual costs against planned progress and costs. System costs that get out of hand can further render the expert system to the unloved and poorly supported investment classification of software systems.

The planned benefits expected from the system should be the responsibility of the potential users. They should be made to quantify and otherwise enumerate the benefits of the system as they see it. After all, they are the ones who will have to realise the perceived benefits — so they had better be very clear as to what they want.

Every project operates according to some *timetable* as should the expert system project. The timetable set should be conservative and should allow for an acceptable level of flexibility. It should plan for goals and sub-goals to be reached and the entire project plan should be submitted to writing.

## 15.2 THE PROJECT MANAGER

The project manager can be either a member of the technology department, a representative of the users, or someone actively independent. What matters most is that he has an active interest in the project and that it is not just considered to be another task on his plate. He needs to be familiar with the concept of expert systems and particularly with the objectives of the system for which he has been appointed project manager. He needs to display objectivity in the way he manages the project. If he or his department has a vested interest in the development of the system he cannot allow this to cloud his handling of the project or his interaction with other members of the application team. Any discipline or pressure that he wishes to apply needs to be considered as fair by those involved. It will be to his distinct advantage if he has a good understanding of the domain area in which the system is to operate as well as being experienced in the operation of the other systems in the organisation with which the expert system may be potentially integrated

Project organisation is important. The project manager needs to have good organisational abilities as well as the tenacity and perseverance to manage a relatively unexplored area for most organisations namely, that of expert systems.

## 15.3 STAGES OF EXPERT SYSTEM DEVELOPMENT

In broad terms there are usually ten steps to the development of an expert system from conceptualisation to eventual user acceptance and ongoing maintenance.

1. **Outline specification.** This stage includes the activities of identifying an appropriate system; conceptualisation by the expert and the knowledge engineer as to the concepts, boundaries, relationships and control mechanisms to be included in the system. Development strategies and constraints as well as user expectations are explored. The results of this stage of assessing the potential performance and benefits of the system should be encapsulated in an outline specification. This specification will hold for the initial prototype development.

2. **Knowledge acquisition.** During this stage, both the expert and the knowledge engineer will be involved in intensive interaction. The expert will

be intent in articulating his knowledge in line with the constraints imposed as well as trying to highlight the essential issues that set the information apart as being knowledge. As was mentioned earlier, know-how distinguishes the expert from the novice — and this must come through in the expert system. The knowledge engineer on the other hand will be trying to come to grips with the essence of the knowledge, its limits and complexities.

3. **Knowledge representation.** Once the knowledge engineer has a fair grasp of the shape that the system might take, its content and its limits, he is faced with the task of designing a method for appropriate knowledge representation. This is a very important part of the project. A successful system that meets user requirements, will do so only if the knowledge of the expert is conveyed in a manner understandable to users and in a fashion congruent with the way the expert normally solves problems. It is the knowledge engineer's ability to enter into the frame of reference of both the expert and the potential users and to take the knowledge acquired and suitably structure it, that will set him apart as a good or bad engineer.

During this phase both the expert and the knowledge engineer will be actively involved in building the system and testing the rule base as it emerges. After a period, the knowledge acquisition stage and the knowledge representation will merge into one as the prototyping starts gathering speed.

4. **Prototype development.** As soon as the expert and the knowledge engineer have established some guidelines as to how the system is likely to emerge, the prototyping stage will begin. Most system developments proceed by developing a prototype model prior to establishing a detailed system specification in anticipation of a full blown system.

The advantage of developing a prototype system first is that the application team, notably the expert and the knowledge engineer, can establish whether the system is feasible. Further, users get an opportunity to test out the system and to see whether it is likely to meet their requirements. It also provides the application team with an opportunity to evaluate the accrual of costs and the performance of the chosen software.

A skilled knowledge engineer and a motivated and experienced expert can build a prototype system within a number of weeks. Herein lies a great psychological advantage. A reasonably workable system that is produced within a short space of time instils confidence in all concerned. Confidence is the most valuable ingredient of all!

5. **Main knowledge acquisition.** Once the prototype system has been reviewed and tested by the application team, procedures are normally established for the development of the full blown system. The first stage here is again to assess the extent of the knowledge that is required in order to meet user needs. During this stage it may be decided to involve multiple experts in the acquisition process. It is also an appropriate time to consider whether the system can, or should be integrated with other systems existent

within the organisation. The overlap of the knowledge with other areas within the organisation might need to be more fully explored as well as the other interfaces, both manual and machine.

6. **Detailed specification.** The application team develops a detailed specification during this phase. Some aspects of the expert system will face scrutiny from first principles while others will be developed as a consequence of the lessons learned during the prototyping phase. The detailed specification will also cover the objectives of the expanded system; the resources required; the projected time; planned costs; system testing and implementation planning.

7. **System development.** This is likely to take a sizeable portion of the entire project time allocated. The efficacy of the project manager will become evident during this stage, as will the commitment of the entire project team. During this stage it is vitally important that users know well how the system is progressing, any problems being encountered, the evidence of new limitations and new opportunities. Their support during this phase will be critical to the performance of the expert(s) and the knowledge engineer. As this is the phase with the greatest investment in both time and costs, this stage requires the most careful monitoring.

8. **Testing and validation.** It is very important to the success and acceptability of the expert system that it is subjected to rigorous testing prior to hand over to users. This testing takes several forms. Firstly the knowledge and the consequent rule base needs to be validated. This is most often achieved by obtaining the co-operation of other experts and representatives of the users. The wider the intended use of the system, the larger the number of potential users and the greater the number of interfaces, the more intense the required testing of the system.

The capability of the software in delivering the necessary features of the system also needs testing. The dependability of the system will embrace checking that the knowledge base is appropriate and that the system is working as it should. Although the expert system is not expected to be 100 per cent right all of the time, its success rate needs to be at least as high as that of an experienced expert in the domain area.

*Implementation*
Implementation covers the last two stages of expert system development.

9. **Implementation itself.** In this aspect expert systems do not differ from other software systems in any significant way. Where they do perhaps differ from conventional systems is in their approach to problems. This fact in itself calls for more detailed and carefully spelled out implementation procedures. Though the resistance to change factor should have been well ironed out before reaching this stage, in reality this cannot be guaranteed. Implementation procedures should be user led and user supported to be

successful. The implementation plan should have been documented during the Detailed Specification stage. Once again the project manager will be tested with regard to his ability to manage this process.

10. **Maintenance.** An expert system needs to be maintained as a live system. This means that it requires continuous revision and updating to ensure that the knowledge is always up to date and appropriate to the changing environment in which organisations operate. Maintenance procedures should be formally documented and the responsibility therefore should be assigned in advance. Once the experts lose interest in maintaining the system the users will lose interest in using it.

## 15.4   THE RESPONSIBILITY OF MANAGEMENT

Management should take an active interest in following the course of the expert system's development. It should take responsibility for monitoring progress, applying pressure when required and providing motivational support when it appears warranted. The greatest complexity in expert system development is that it is a new concept, relying on new types of skills and developed with new (developmental) software systems. While newness can be appealing, it can also bring with it trepidation and scepticism.

# Part IV

## The Future

The uncertainty with regard to the future is especially true in the world of science and technology. The pace at which the world changes in these areas can be viewed as both exciting and alarming. As man finds better things to do, and better ways in which to do them, he sets new horizons and casts away old ideas about himself and his environment. Whether progress is always a good thing is a highly debatable point. Many might argue that scientific advance has left a certain amount of social destruction in its wake. This could be because a lot of scientific discovery leads us to do things which could be classified as not normal or congruent to man's make-up.

The development of expert systems has been largely stimulated by the desire, by some, to analyse and then to improve upon our thinking processes. The end result should be an advancement in the way we think and make decisions. Few would argue that this endeavour is anything but laudable. The resistance lies mainly in the apparently increased dependence on the machine as the primary work, and growing social, interface for man. While the use of machines is *almost* accepted as the norm for supporting manual and mechanical processes, supporting *thinking* processes, and even augmenting these is a new ball game altogether. Thinking is for (most) humans a very natural process.

One would hope that the research and effort applied to improving our thought processes, by assisting us to make better quality decision, will not have any negative side effects. There are of course no guarantees, but this could certainly be viewed as one of our more healthy pursuits. One thing we can be sure of is that there are many devoted to the advance in this area, so advance we will!

## MANAGEMENT AND THE FUTURE

Management effort is largely devoted to the future. It can do a limited amount about the present and nothing about the past. It needs to try to anticipate the future and to prepare for it. Management science sometimes calls this environmental scanning, scenario planning or strategic planning. These exercises are devoted to analysing how the future might shape the macro and micro environment and how the organisation might best respond thereto. Forward looking management takes the view that they are part of the future and, as much as they should prepare a suitable response, they should also aim to influence the future to their advantage. Playing an active role in shaping the future enhances the power of the organisation. This can usually only be achieved if management is prepared to invest in the present with the objective of receiving above average future returns. This requires foresight and well informed risk-taking. This means that management is required to extend its horizons, to sacrifice today's returns for tomorrow's, and generally to take a longer-term view.

The evidence of the success of this approach abounds. It is clear that the trend has been set and that organisations are extending their sights and planning for the ten-year rather than the one or three-year time-scale.

The view that we are moving towards a knowledge-based society supports the sentiment that there will be reappraisal of expert knowledge destined to receive new recognition and thus a new premium.

## COMPETITIVE ADVANTAGE AND THE FUTURE

The fierce competition that exists in most industries is forecast to proceed at an unabated pace. Increasing polarisation in most industries is resulting in enormous multinational organisations with extensive distribution networks, as compared with small niche operators that compete in narrower and more exclusive target markets.

The new competition is taking the form of collaborative agreements both inter- and intra-industry. Licensing, distribution and joint venture arrangements are just some of the ways in which organisations are trying to extend their operational spheres. The larger organisations in particular are more and more dependent on volume business in order to break-even and to achieve acceptable targets of growth. The massive relative increase in fixed costs for many industries is in the majority of instances due to technological advancement. There are few industries left that are impervious to the competitive advantages that can be achieved by using the latest technology. It is predicted by many futurists, economists and politicians that the worldwide trend towards a domination of service industries will gain added momentum. The role of technology in service industries is especially important, and for some sectors, e.g. Financial Services, is the backbone of the product/market offering.

Whether the continued intensity of competition will prove to enhance the world for all stakeholders is a difficult issue unlikely ever to be clarified. Not only are people's perceptions different and biased, but attaining some measure of different perceptions is a wellnigh impossible task — one only has to read the different reports in the media to confirm this point.

What is relevant to management, however, is that gaining and sustaining competitive advantage is going to remain their preoccupation for some time to come, and the more effectively they are able to participate the better the chance of long-term success with serenity.

## TECHNOLOGY AND THE FUTURE

For those who resist technology, the future is certainly bleak in some aspects. Technology is an intrinsic part of our daily lives and is destined to pervade it even further. All our modern day advances are expressed in terms of new technology — whether it be home banking, artificial insemination, educating the blind, Star Wars or treatment for glaucoma, the role of technology plays a vital part.

As was discussed earlier, there are many who wish to participate in the comforts that technology might bring, but adamantly resist its apparent threats. So, while consumer's rush to purchase the cheapest goods from Japan, Taiwan or Korea, workers picket factories to resist downward pressures on wages, upward pressures on productivity and apparent dumping of foreign goods. The great paradox lies in that the workers are the consumers! How will the future resolve this increasing problem?

It is not just the workers who have had to come to terms with the dependence and pervasiveness of technology. Management at all levels are under a certain amount of pressure to involve themselves more actively in the potential use of technology in their organisation. If management does not do this spontaneously competition is likely to be the greatest motivating force.

Technology has found its way into the boardroom in the form of Decision Support Systems, as well as being used extensively by managers at all levels as aids to budgeting and planning. Process technology, which in the past was developing at a faster pace than information technology is now being integrated with the latest form of information technology — namely that of expert systems. Expert systems integrated with computerised machine systems is a new method of developing on line, real time self-corrective quality control systems. Not only will the future systems be capable of diagnosing faults, but they will also be able to take corrective action, to explain the details of the fault and to substantiate the particular correction action taken. The production line will no longer need to be managed apart from the results of its performance. Likewise the advances in information technology will radically improve the reporting methods both within the organisation and that demanded by the outside world.

Although Artificial Intelligence and expert systems were the initial inspiration of the Americans they no longer hold a clear lead in the race to the future. The Japanese and their Fifth Generation Computer programme could well surpass any other known achievements in the near future. The fifth generation computer is designed to process logic with the same speed and proficiency that fourth generation computers process arithmetic. In fact the hopes are that the hardware will be so engineered as to improve on any processing achievements to date and, that the new machines will have enormous amounts of memory at relatively little incremental cost. The new software that will be developed will cope with natural language processing and will be designed to be infinitely more user friendly (so the technologists hope).

The future interfaces will be considered more intelligent as they will be able to listen, see, understand and respond interactively with the user. Technologists predict even greater productivity advancements in every sphere and that decision makers will be able to benefit from the guidance of intelligent human assistants.

## KNOWLEDGE AND THE FUTURE

The author subscribes to the view that we are rapidly moving towards a knowledge-based society. This means that knowledge will become the most important traded commodity and that people will be recognised as knowledge workers. There will be greater emphasis on the *knowledge* that we have, and the way that we are able to apply it, than has been hitherto granted. The new emphasis on being knowledgeable is predicted to change the way we evaluate performance and achievement. Knowledge is a much wider concept than just pure intelligence. There exists many a debate as to whether our current practices of testing and labelling people as intelligent or otherwise are appropriate or even acceptable. The emphasis on a knowledge-based society could mean:

- changed methods of evaluating people performance
- advances in our educational system
- greater emphasis on the process of carrying something through than purely the results
- recognition of knowledge that results from experience or wisdom rather than just from training and education
- an opportunity for greater equality as all people can take some pride in the specific knowledge unique to them

This sounds a highly idealist theory — and of course it is. Plato and Socrates were idealists too as they aspired to an infinitely better world well over 2000 years ago! Is that not still our greatest desire?

## THE ROLE OF EXPERT SYSTEMS IN THE FUTURE

There is a lot of activity in the expert systems market — far more so than one might believe. The reason for this is that many expert system developments are cloaked in secrecy because the sponsoring organisations believe that the system will provide some form of competitive advantage. Expert systems development in the commercial world has been slow in taking off. The major obstacle has, and continues to be, the problem of proving an acceptable return on the required investment in advance of the system development. Although the returns achievable by investing in expert systems will become more evident as people gain experience in harnessing this new tool suitably, this will take time.

Expert system developments in the area of finance have seen the greatest advancements. Most of the larger financial institutions have several individuals involved in exploring the potential opportunities for these systems and many prototypes are currently under development. Some full blown systems are also being used, notably in the areas of foreign exchange exposure management and other investment banking areas.

In those organisations where expert systems are being built there is a wide selection of user involvement. This is a good thing. As we have discussed at length, the success of computer applications lies in user participation and acceptance. Expert systems will increase the usage and dissemination of systems throughout an organisation. This in itself is likely to positively influence the perception of the usages of the technology.

The new technology is aimed at enhancing the capabilities and power of Expert Systems. The new hardware will handle vast numbers of inferences per second which will enable system designers to build larger and larger systems. This will also assist in getting around the combinatorial explosion problem. In the future most full blown expert systems are likely to be built on hardware that has the capability of coping with large systems. While prototype development lends itself to personal computer type developments particularly using expert system shells, the adolescence and maturity of expert systems is destined to manifest itself in the form of integrated, distributed mainframe systems.

With regard to knowledge engineering, already several different schools with different approaches exist. As with management style, there is no one absolutely correct method. The knowledge engineering approach to an application should be viewed in the context of that application. The objectives of the system, the number of users and the nature of the knowledge being represented will all directly affect the style of method to be chosen. Suffice it to say that these schools of thought are likely to spread their wings as applications increase in number and variety. Management needs to be aware that different approaches do exist without getting drawn into the debates that are sure to arise over the advantages and disadvantages of the different methods.

The expanded use of expert systems will advance the performance of people, organisations and even governments. Expert systems will potentially be able to perform inferences faster than humans; to analyse and assimilate enormous amounts of information in the twinkling of an eye; to sort and infer new knowledge from the knowledge in its knowledge base, and to identify new combinations and methods of induction. Those who intend taking advantage of the potential of expert systems at an early stage, albeit at risk initially, are predicted to be ahead of their less visionary competitors. While expert systems are looked upon as the future technological and strategic tool of the next decade, they can still only act as expert support and *not* substitution for sound management practices inspired by a concerned, enlightened and well motivated management team.

# Bibliography

Ayer, A. J., *The Problem of Knowledge*, Pelican Books, 1986.

Beerel, A. C., *The Realities of Raising Business Finance*. A practical guide, Management Update, 1986.

Bennis, W. — Nanus, B., *Leaders — The Strategies for Taking Charge*, Harper & Row, New York, 1985.

Berkeley, G., *The Principle of Human Knowledge*, Fontana Press, 1962.

Chorafas, D. N., *Applying Expert Systems in Business*, McGraw-Hill, 1987.

Cornford, F. M., *Plato's Theory of Knowledge*, Routledge & Kegan Paul, 1979.

De Bono, E., *'Tactics'. The Art and Science of Success*, Fontana/Collins, 1985.

Enals, R., *Artificial Intelligence Applications to Logical Reasoning and Historical Research*, Ellis Horwood, 1986.

Feigenbaum, E. A. & McCorduck, P., *The Fifth Generation. Artificial Intelligence and Japan's Computer Challenge to the World*, Pan Books, 1983, 1984.

Forsyth, R. & Rada, R., *Machine Learning, Applications in Expert Systems and Information Technology*, Ellis Horwood, 1986.

Goldsmith, W. & Clutterbuck, D., *The Winning Streak*, Weidenfeld & Nicolson, London, 1984.

Hewett, J. & d'Auvale, G., *Commercial Expert Systems in Europe*, Ovum Ltd, 1986.

Hickman, C. R. & Silva, M. A., *Creating Excellence*, George Allen & Unwin, London, 1984.

Higgins, J. M., *Strategy — Formulation, Implementation and Control*, The Dryden Press, 1985.

ICAWE & BIM, *Investment Appraisal, Finance for Managers*, Vol. 6, Gee & Co., 1985.

*The Knowledge Engineer Review* (a quarterly journal), Imperial Cancer Research Fund Laboratories, Lincoln's Inn Fields, London WC2A 3PX.

Maslow, A. H., *Motivation and Personality*, Harper & Row, 1970.

Ohmae, K., *The Mind of the Strategist. The Art of Japanese Business*, McGraw-Hill, 1982.

Peters, T. J. & Waterman, R. H. Jnr, *In Search of Excellence*, Harper & Row, New York, 1982.

Porter, M. E., *Competitive Strategy*, The Free Press, New York, 1980.

Rappaport, A. (ed.), *Information for Decision Making*, Prentice-Hall, 1975.

Schutte, F. G., *Integrated Management Systems*, Butterworths, 1981.

Sell, P. S., *Expert Systems — A Practical Introduction*, Macmillan, 1985.

Slatter, P. E., *Building Expert Systems: Cognitive Emulation*, Ellis Horwood, 1987.

Slurai, Y. & Tsujii, J., *Artificial Intelligence, Concepts, Techniques and Applications*, John Wiley, 1986.

Sprague, R. H. Jnr, & Watson, H. J. (eds), *Decision Support Systems, Putting Theory into Practice*, Prentice-Hall, 1986.

Torrance, S. (ed.), *The Mind and the Machine, Philosophical Aspects of Artificial Intelligence*, Ellis Horwood, 1984.

Turner, M., *Expert Systems: A Management Guide*, PA Computers and Telecommunications, 1985.

Vennis, W. & Namus, B., *Leaders — The Strategies for Taking Change*, Harper & Row, New York, 1985.

Waterman, D. A., *A Guide to Expert Systems*, Addison-Wesley, 1986.

Yazdani, M. & Narayanan, A. (eds), *Artificial Intelligence: Human Effects*, Ellis Horwood, Chichester, 1984.

Zorkogy, P., *Information Technology — An Introduction*, Pitman, 1985.

# Index